I Found My Tomorrow in Paris

A Memoir

Marilyn Pearsol Giorgetti

ISBN-13: 978-1535484527

ISBN-10: 1535484527

Library of Congress Control Number: 2016916403

CreateSpace Independent Publishing Platform, North Charleston, SC

Contents

For Leo

As with a book the pages of life turn rapidly, and I find myself in a new and different world, with only remembrances of the moments of long ago.

Author's note

Sometimes we are the last to realize what our souls are starved for. Or maybe we do know, but we're too fearful to risk what is safe and dependable for the challenging unknown. Sometimes life needs to turn on us to get us moving and considering risking everything.

Beyond the shores of my reality, where for three decades I faithfully performed my role as wife and mother, another realm awaited me. A realm of ancient history and personal discovery, of architectural grandeur and intellectual broadening. But in the daily patterns of my earlier years such an exploration into who I really was and what all I was capable of accomplishing was not at the forefront of my thoughts.

In the 1950s, my life was simple and grew only to a shelved status culturally determined for girls who married soon out of high school. This cup consigned to me kept filled without much ado really; never overflowing, it merely teased at the lip. But life that centered round home and hearth contented me, satisfied as I was deemed to be with what I'd now describe as a homogenized expectation for women in that period of American life. It wasn't until my divorce and a trip to South America that I was awakened to the possibilities of more. South America had captivated me with its beauty, its exotic bouquets of people and sounds, colors and scents. Returning home then, the grass felt more alive between my bare toes, just as it had in the days of my youth. Clouds were no longer inching overhead. They hastened now, as if dashing for some longed-for destiny. Fog rolled in with determination, shrouding the hillside below my coastal home. It settled so thick beneath my deck I felt I could walk out into forever. If I would just take the step I would come face to face with whatever was out there that beckoned me. And something was beckoning. I yearned for more. But more of what?

For several years more I clung to 'safe' and 'dependable,' until it all evaporated like a dream at first light. Yet my overturned world did not leave me without options; oddly, it presented me with a persuasive opportunity. A journey, as it would turn out, that would be my true coming of age, my second flowering.

Nice 1985

M y courage throttles down as the engines pull back for our descent into Nice. No one is here to meet me. Am I really ready for this? Back in the states I'd built myself up as this brave heroine prepared to conquer the European world. Now I'm quaking in my boots.

I put my face up to the oval window. The sky is clear. *So much for the forecasted snow*. It couldn't be a bluer sky for February. *An omen*?

The plane descends into the view. A line of blue-green palm trees appears to be baking in the sun. Through the window across the aisle I see more stately trees standing tall against an azure Mediterranean Sea. I cup my mouth to keep the thrill from leaping out of me. All these months imagining such heights, and here I am just seconds from stepping down into my new reality. I feel the *whump* of wheels touch down and everyone applauds, including me. Gliding along the tarmac all I can whisper is, "Okay, God, you got me this far."

3

The hatch is open, and as I pause on the landing a blast of freezing air embraces me. I pull the lapels of my woefully inadequate coat up close around my neck and step out, looking to the sky triumphant. Slowly then, as I want to savor this moment, I descend the portable steps to the tarmac and revel in my arrival in Nice. Outside the loading zone, however, I have to jump up and down and hug myself to ward off the penetrating freeze. Okay, so it's really, really cold. But I'm here!

Finally inside a rather cozy cab and zipping along the outskirts of Nice, the driver speeds along the boulevard adjacent to the *Promenade des Anglais.* The late afternoon sun dangles, almost hesitant, as if awaiting my permission to settle into the sea. And that is just fine with me.

Blocks of multi-storied apartment buildings hunker to my left, each with grand-shuttered windows closed off for now—must be waiting for summer visitors. I've beaten the tourist crowd. Then just as we pass the famous and magnificent Hôtel Negresco, the taxi hooks left and squeaks its way down a narrow, spiraling street and stops in front of a nondescript hotel. Heady with anticipation, I make haste to check in and deposit my luggage, to begin my adventure. Too excited earlier to think of food, there is no denying now the pangs of hunger clawing at my stomach.

Nearby the hotel is a *brasserie* with a fogged-up window. I go in, find a small booth, order a sandwich, and savor the unfamiliar sights. Melodic conversations emanate from neighboring tables, and I wonder: will I ever sound like them? I relish the prospect as I inhale my snack, bid *au revoir* to the waiter, then back to my stroll toward downtown.

Daylight is swiftly dissolving into dusk, while a fog (or mist) hovers over antiquated street lamps. My adrenalin pumps wildly as daylight surrenders to all the little shops, who, one by one, are glowing now with golden warmth. I should be exhausted, but I refuse to entertain the thought of sleep. It's as if my feet have a mission and I am merely along for the ride. Not just me, others too have filled the sidewalks. Residents, I imagine. Though from all the chatter I'm not the only foreigner.

Each step toward Avenue Jean Médecin, the main thoroughfare, brings me closer to music and laughter, shouting, drums and horns. *A parade?* Weaving on toward the sounds through a thin current of pedestrians, a cluster of noisy revelers in crazy masks and colorful costumes head straight toward me. Their shoulders bump me and pull me into their flow, until I am encircled by their whirlwind of merriment. In their raised hands are cans, which they point at me. Colorful, stringy ooze shoots through the brisk air and covers my head and arms. Laughing, I flail my arms up wildly to ward off this intrusion. To no avail. Squiggly ribbons dangle over my eyes and trail down the front of me. Just as swiftly then, their whirlwind vanishes into the crowd behind me. *What on earth?*

"It's the last night of *Carnaval*," a stranger informs me. Electric gaiety has so charged the air, I think that if I turn too quickly I may just set off sparks. But I can't help getting caught up in all the laughter and celebrating. I feel like a kid twirling and dancing and marching in sync with this growing throng of celebrants.

Down the center of the street Big Heads with giant, garishly painted faces parade past me, mingling with colorful and outrageous floats, troupes of dancers and jugglers. So close I can reach out and touch them. Hundreds of pasteboard caricatures dance and prance from one side of the boulevard to the other, and here I am, unbelievably in the midst of it all. The Nice *Carnaval.*

Bang! Bang! Pop, pop, pop. Fireworks explode in the sky, as thousands of upturned faces transform into newly saved penitents. A sea breeze carries the scent of cordite, as diminishing embers flicker downward and vanish. From the scaffolding, above the stacks of bleachers that line the street, more big-headed and outlandishly-illuminated figures peer down at me. It's as if they too are observing this extravaganza. Children squealing with excitement compounds this bizarre happening, welcoming me to France in the greatest way. Unbelievable, that I am witnessing this spectacular celebration so soon after setting foot in Nice.

Time has escaped me. It's early morning and still dark, as I stumble back to my hotel and board its tiny birdcage-like elevator. I lean my tired body against its frail frame, not wanting to release the exhilaration. The lift groans skyward defying the pull of gravity. Deposited on the correct floor I exit into the hallway, locate my room, and crash on a double-swayback, chenille-covered bed. And yet it seems I am not destined to sleep this last bit of night, my first in this faraway land.

Out in the hall the iron elevator door clanks shut. Hotel room doors slam. But it is the booming laughter and bellows of *whoops* that jolt me wide awake. Sailors, apparently. Probably stationed in Marseilles and taking their leave. I imagine them celebrating and have no other choice but to lie awake, until they have their fill of whatever they're imbibing and lose consciousness. As I lie there unable to surrender to blissful sleep, in an unbelievable state of awareness, I ponder the long road that has brought me here.

Laguna Beach, 1982

O ur view. My husband, Johnny, and I discovered this beach enclave just south of Laguna Beach in 1965, its pristine beauty and innocence still intact. We reveled in the availability of the sandy nook shaped like a half moon protected by large outcroppings of rock to the north and south. Where land meets the ocean an invisible hand had carved into the shoreline and formed a secluded cove for sunbathing and swimming. Homes perched high on bluffs luxuriate in the unparalleled sights and sounds of feral surf pounding the rocks below; while on the more docile cove a colorful buoy of a crab fisherman bobs tirelessly, waiting for the next boat to arrive, to retrieve its bounty from the ocean.

"It's too bad Johnny couldn't be here to share this life and this home we built," I said. After an afternoon outing with my close friend, Ali, and another not-so-close friend, Diana, the three of us had just returned to my home in Laguna

Beach. This was an unusual occurrence, as I typically work while they do not, though my customers' schedules do afford me a tad of freedom now and then to play hooky, to sit here today in my living room with our glasses of Pinot Grigio and enjoy the ocean view. And though the comment had slipped out into the air between us, I'd said it mostly to myself really. And being sensitive and rather emotional, tearing up at the slightest provocation (like when I hear the National Anthem), I did just that. Diana took one stern look at me and suggested I see a counselor for my depression.

"What…what depression? Over an amicable divorce I initiated? I assure you I'm fine, Diana. Just making a comment, sharing my thoughts. It's just sad, that's all." How could she understand the friendship that Johnny and I had and, after 30 years, still have? How could she know what heartbreaking reasons had led to my decision? Neither of us was at fault. We just couldn't fix it. But Diana persists and suggests I see her father, a psychologist, mind you, "who just happens to be coming out for a visit with my mother." Diana and I are not close. Like I said, it's Ali and I who are dear friends. But I know that Diana was divorced and has since remarried. Maybe she experienced depression. Nevertheless I've accepted the reality. It's just over.

"Maybe you should, Marilyn," Ali joins in, like she's part of what's now become a conspiracy to convince me of some deep-seeded depression. She sits across from me in my living room and insists I am repressing my feelings. For Pete's sake. I am not depressed. Of all people, Ali should know this, as we talk almost every day. *Coping* might be a better word. My divorce was not the end of the world. I'm adjusting and in a good place now, but I would feel even better if my best friend wasn't siding with…

I glance at Diana, who sits regally on my sofa, and suddenly resent her insensitive presence. But Ali, my friend of many years, how can she betray me like this in front of someone who I feel would not have my back if I needed it? I let it go. It's an awkward few minutes, but heaven forbid I should have a confrontation in my own living room. I see where this comrades-in-arms thing is going. There's no point in continuing. To restore some courtesy and avoid an afternoon-turned-train wreck, I agree to talk to her father. It doesn't mean I will. At this time I have no desire to talk to a psychologist.

Diana decided to throw a party for her parents that included her entourage of friends. She has the perfect home for entertaining with its central glass-enclosed patio and a fire that crackles and warms from a round, raised pit. But it is the details of my not-so-inconsequential meeting with her father that night that stays with me.

"I'm happy to meet you," I greet the man, a Red Buttons look-alike. I tell him that Diana suggested I talk with him about a personal matter of mine. There is a definite smugness about him, but I brush it off. *Diana has not fallen far from the tree.* Maybe it's just me. I mention my divorce and how I think I have traversed that slope with ease, how rather good I've been feeling about my decision and don't see anything abnormal about it, but does he? He suggests we go to some place quieter. It's the first sound I've heard from him. Much to my dismay and discomfort he takes my elbow and guides me away from the sounds and animations of the other guests into the presently-isolated center atrium, which no longer feels warm and cozy. Like a wind-up toy, the man suddenly becomes rather chatty about his trip here to the West Coast that he and his wife have just made. I'm trying to be polite, but I don't think he's heard one word I said. Still chatting

9

away, he rambles about other unrelated drivel. *That's it. This was a mistake.* Then just as I am about to excuse myself, his watery gaze swoops down along the V of my neckline. It's all the cue I need. I wish him an enjoyable vacation and can't return to the party quick enough. During the evening I bump into Diana and mention that I met her dad. That's all that transpires between us. But her dad? Red Buttons just happens to be near the front entryway, his wife right next to him, when it comes time to retrieve my coat and purse. Much to my chagrin, he takes my coat and, proprietarily, he helps me on with it. He opens the door for me and I walk out.

Now, the day before this party, Diana and I had arranged for me to come back the morning after to pick up some decorator pillows. However, no one ever answered her doorbell. I checked my day calendar: *10:00 a.m. Diana.* I figured she must've forgotten, her parents being there and all. No big deal. I left, and the party was the last time she and I spoke to each other. In fact, calls from our group of friends have stopped altogether for days now. Except for Ali. She calls to keep in touch. Like today. She's called to tell me how the girls had recently met for lunch and, why wasn't I there? Because I wasn't invited, I tell her. I try to brush it aside, but to not be invited means something is wrong. The thought of them excluding me… Ali continues to chatter, but my thoughts shift back to having been so warmly invited to Diana's party, then stood up on her doorstep the following morning, to this sudden shunning. My stomach twists. Something is wrong, but what?

In the weeks since Diana's party I've just been working diligently out of necessity and escape. Customers once rushing to buy real estate have slowed to a dribble. We're especially feeling the drought of this possible recession, though the government is still refusing to call it a recession. 1982 will be remembered, as we are certainly heading into another depression if things don't change soon.

Earlier in my career customers were buying real estate and selling the following year for a great profit. It didn't take a bop on the head to figure out I could be doing the same thing, so I started investing. How satisfying, watching my investments turn around so easily. I would put the minimum down, rent out the property and sell it the following year. My investments were expanding. But now, with the economy plunging and everyone's afraid to spend…if it wasn't for this one soon-to-turn-around transaction (it will more than get my finances up and gliding in the black)…I don't even want to think about how over-leveraged I've gotten myself. I hear the phone, it's probably Ali.

"Hello, Marilyn? Bob here. Listen, I hate to do this to you, but we gotta stop everything right now." I have several customers, but I know instantly who this is and exactly what is at stake. Bob's is the million-dollar transaction, cash purchase, 30-day escrow I've been banking on. I feel myself strangling the phone like it's this guy's hand, and if I let it go I'll drown. I'm speechless. My silence, I'm sure, prompts him to further convince me to cut him loose. "Disney stock nosedived. I've got bundles. *Had* a bundle. It's gone, Marilyn." *Like saying my name should make this easier?* Pleading. "If I don't get out of this now with you I'm ruined. I mean it, I'm about to lose everything. " *He's* going to lose everything? I'm looking at serious losses. This guy doesn't need a second home; this property is galaxies from being a necessity for him. But I have a $35,000 second mortgage due yesterday. A Disney stock dive. Not once in seven years of selling real estate has something like this happened to me. It's not like I had other investments to fall back on, but my livelihood is solely real estate.

11

I wonder if he can hear my sigh of resignation. There is no way I cannot honor Bob's wishes.

In a daze I go to the kitchen and pour myself a glass of wine, head back into the living room, sip my Pinot Grigio and stand gazing out at the horizon. Here I'd thought it would be safe to gamble on our pricey Southern California coast: "These are the golden years—the '70s—property values can only go up." Ha! Well, I've no one to blame really but myself. Had I diversified and squirrelled away enough cash to prevent something like this... I force myself to think about anything else, but Bob's plea to 'pull out' keeps interrupting like a party line.

I continue sipping, savoring the wine's relaxing affect, and wonder—of all things—when the knot first began to unravel between Johnny and me. An upsurge of old memory pulls me into its grasp and carries me. I am sixteen. My brother has just come home from the Navy with his friend, Johnny. Johnny is cute and friendly and ends up staying at our home while he attends college. Very quickly we become good friends, someone is interested in me. This is huge. Having to adhere to my parents' conservative, fundamental beliefs while in high school makes me feel inadequate, so different from my peers, and in my thinking, unlovable and, undateable. Soon after high school Johnny asks me to marry him. It is *de rigeur* to be pinned or engaged by graduation, and even though my parents want me to enroll at a Bible college, they give me their blessing. I am not about to become an old maid. For the first time in my life I go against their wishes. But at nineteen I can't possibly predict the path my decision will take. Nor do I care. I want only to marry Johnny and have his babies. I have just read Galbraith's *Cheaper by the Dozen*. What could be more wonderful than that? Isn't this what we are programed for—get married and have children? A few years pass, but our budding friendship never flowers into passion. What chance for the flame to burn when the spark is smothered by indifference? Life inexorably continues and a son is born. Then a daughter. Over the years, being bereft of emotional bonding takes its toll. The continued absence of intimate affection leaves me wondering, then fearing, is this what marriage is? Years later, our teenage daughter sees my extreme distress. In return, I see how my pain is seriously affecting her. Still more time passes between Johnny and me, until after 30 years and nothing can salvage our bond. By now we no longer have any mutual plans. Our dreams and desires for the future have long since fallen out of sync. There are none. If either of us is ever to find happiness divorce is unavoidable. No amount of introspection and self-analysis seems able to erase the sense of failure and loss I continue to harbor. There never was another in our lives to tear apart our vows. We were just two virgin souls who never should have married. This never was about me—this avoidance or absence of passion. I know that. But so much damage has been done that I return time again to feeling undesirable. Even with my acceptance of the truth it continues to intrude. Time to let it go.

A cold wind surges against my living room sliders. Glancing across the now-darkened surface, I see whitecaps dotting the sea. An autumn front is whipping things up down there, and superimposed against fast-approaching clouds—ablaze now in orangey-hot pink—the features of Catalina Island are melding into a silhouette. Nostalgia pulls me into the expansive view. Our view.

I've stayed as busy as the trickle of customers has dictated since Bob's call a couple months back now. Meanwhile, like slow-tumbling dominos my assets have managed to tortuously collapse.

First, I was forced to sell a cabin at Lake Tahoe, which was really an investment for my son. Then my future retirement Mediterranean condo in Laguna Niguel; the condo overlooks the developing golf course and ocean. Finally, my rental condo in Irvine reverted to the lender. Overnight it seems I've been slammed to the bottom and am unable to get my footing. Each morning I feel such dread and failure, struggling to maintain some financial stability and respectability. This is certainly not where I intended to be at this stage in my life. All these years I've toed a careful line to create a productive work life, comfortable and rewarding. Now only torpor, a lethargy moves like a death angel through me. I feel it. Even my relations with Ali are strained, as my patience and friendship wane with her betrayal. Yet, she continues to keep me abreast with the newest gossip. I dread her calls now.

"I thought you would want to know what they're all saying" (our group of friends). Now, why would I want to know? And has she thought once to defend me? No. She's avoided it for fear she too will be ostracized.

And the shunning continues.

To think clearly and extricate myself from this chaos seems impossible. I try to make light of it, and normally I can bring sunshine with me wherever I go. But lately, it's like I'm under an unremitting cloud. And the more I think about this cloud honestly, the more I realize it's been lingering for some time. A few months? A year? Longer? I shake my head. This can't be about Johnny. The divorce was so amicable, even the process was devoid of negativity. And once the papers were signed and everything was settled, Johnny willingly agreed to let me buy his share of the house. I wanted the house. It was the one unbroken thing that embodied all that was good between us. But with everything falling apart now, having the house seems a hollow victory. Speaking of which, here I thought at least I'd still have Ali to talk with. I miss having Ali as a friend. But at last a phone call from her—our last. Today she informed me that my meeting with Diana's father had caused a rift between him and his wife, and that they'd packed up and left the following morning. *Diana is blaming me?* I'm the culprit. The home wrecker. I'm furious that Ali did not remind Diana that she was the one who'd suggested the meeting. I could no longer trust Ali. Did I need friends so desperately that I just closed my eyes to who I was becoming? I couldn't care less about social standing and prestige. Whatever possessed me to so readily fall in step with them? I see Diana's face. I hear her and Ali pressing me to meet with Diana's father. Why didn't I stand my ground? My stomach churns. How in the world do I fight gossip? Try as I do, I cannot come up with a strategy. I feel my energy and drive draining out of me and I only know that things will never be the same around here. The gossip on top of my divorce, my financial world crumbling—*I have to pull myself together.* But do I just continue on at the office with its unrelenting pace and demanding positive front, like nothing's wrong? I'm just so exhausted just thinking about it. And I'm so, so sad that Johnny and I didn't have the tools to make things work.

All that has long been welling up finds liberation.

2

Eventually, I sold my home that overlooks the ocean. With the proceeds I moved my things into a rental condo in Laguna and bought a commercial property as an investment. But I have no energy to use this property and start again from scratch. There must be something out there for me to succeed at, but what? And what is success? All I ever wanted was to be at peace and be happy. Lately, all my attempts have been futile. I find myself seeking help from another source. It's not like God and I have been close, just acquaintances. But now I need His help to work through this and pull myself together.

I roll off my bed, find a pen and my journal from the desk and climb back in between the blankets. *Dear God...* The worries of late, my requests for guidance through—and deliverance from—the chaos that continues to smolder... More words than I can keep up with are loosed and flowing across the pages.

Journaling is becoming my nightly ritual. Through this process of writing down my thoughts and feelings I'm beginning to see how my life has been running rudderless. It seems I've been on a long voyage to nowhere. There are other things too, small things, not jelling in my life. In total, it all feels insurmountable. If it wasn't for the words of wisdom coming to me recently, early in the mornings, even in the middle of the night sometimes—like rescuing pieces of driftwood over the depths of my concerns—I'd succumb to this emotional undertow. The words come so fast I must retrieve them before they float away.

Because I couldn't continue living in turmoil I agreed to see a pastor a co-worker had recommended. I saw how he'd lightened her burdens and knew I couldn't endure this one alone. In my few visits already he's been patiently guiding me along to where, recently, the dam finally broke, soaking the front of his shirt. There was no stopping my tears, releasing all my pent-up frustrations, anger and resentment. Relief is breaking through. And after entreating God these past weeks, incredibly, I feel like He's responding. A lightness and clarity is breaking through. I believe in Divine intervention, and here I am being intervened upon. God has my back, I know it.

In my journaling I'm dredging up questions from the remotest corners of my recollections. The more I question, the more I discover about myself. I've also been reading a few self-help books. Gradually, my downward spiral is starting to right itself. I couldn't be more encouraged. A meager current of energy is recharged. *At last a measure of hope.*

For no significant reason one morning the sunlight catches my eye with how deliberately it angles into my room. I step into its warmth and pause, and it feels as if someone is standing with me. *Go away for six months.* The words in my head could not have been clearer. Can this be happening? It's as if a beacon has split the sky and whispers for me to follow. Another day I might easily discard the thought. Is this coincidence? Honestly, I've just put down Anne Morrow Lindbergh's *Gift from the Sea,* and the significance of her words could not be better timed:

> The morning of one's life is filled with youth, activity,
> and material success. When we come to the afternoon of our
> life do we attempt to push back the clock to prolong our
> morning? It is not possible to compete with youth. Let the
> afternoon come, and with it a second flowering.

A second chance at life at my age? I'm not some young college student. This isn't the time to embark on a new career. I've got to consider time, my life is half over. Yes, but I'm certainly not dying on the vine. I'm only 55, still young. My spirit cries out to create and seed my second garden and watch it grow. I need my tomorrow. I need to create a new tomorrow. *Go away for six months.* Quiet elation courses through me. The edict could not be more certain. Yes, I'll go away. Far away. Any country will do, it doesn't matter.

After looking at different destinations, and because Nice—much like Laguna —has the same picturesque coastline and climate, France is my destination. I want to get far, far away. I want—I need—to create a new tomorrow, and France is my opening.

For weeks, I've been entertaining all the *what-if*s, and the likelihood of this actually happening is leaning heavily on the positive side. That dark place I was in feels somewhat distant. There is still so much to accomplish, but I am exploring all the avenues toward that goal. So convinced of this new opening, I'm certain that this proverbial light will see me through. For now though, I must keep it to myself. I forbid any negative thoughts from dashing the birth of my embryonic plans. Not one smidgeon of doubt is going to ruin their success.

As I've been going about secretly outlining my escape, each newly discovered solution to a potential obstacle heightens the momentum. I keep weighing the possibilities and the ramifications of this unconventional idea and, week by week, the move is looking more feasible. I am single. My parents are thriving. My two children are grown. I'll need to sell my last property, and really I'm just taking a vacation. A longer than usual vacation. I don't know what awaits me across the Atlantic, but the excitement is fizzing up inside me. Why did I wait so long to step out and chart a new course?

I let my imaginings blossom and empower me with confidence—which is shaky right now—but I must find the core of my own truth. I've already lived someone else's truth, what others expected of me. How early on the feelings of inadequacy fueled the need to prove something and resulted in such vacant goals, eventually I've become someone I never wanted to be. But since my decision to make this journey, I can feel my ego gradually losing its power, exposing the facade of a false life. How high I've been riding for years, enjoying the baubles of a materialistic existence, while an authentic life full of love has bypassed me. Indeed, is a life of fulfillment and peace possible? I have to find out.

To excel now is the answer. But I'm still not telling a single soul. Not yet. No one is going to suck this new wind from my sails. And so far, staying silent has immunized me from all the what-ifs from family and friends who wish they had the courage or freedom to run off on such an outlandish adventure.

Months of silence have snuck by, as the pieces have been falling almost effortlessly into place. Bigger than life the time for departure is coming up. My excitement is ready to burst. Ready to release a lifetime of suppressed dreams and unspent emotions. But even now I can't allow one morsel of negativity for fear my pyramid of hope will collapse.

Emerging like a streak of sunshine on a bleak day, I received a buyer for my commercial property and my acceptance into the University of Nice *Faculté des Lettres* program. It's happening! Turning back is no longer an option. Time to apply for a six-month visa.

Also, in order to live in France long-term I'll need to show employment or adequate funds for the duration of my stay. No bank in Laguna has the capacity to wire funds to Nice, so I'll have to drive to Beverly Hills, a two-hour drive up and back. I will pay off all my outstanding debts from the proceeds of my commercial property and invest in a CD. At 10% interest that'll work. Each month I'll wire the funds from my bank to the bank in Beverly Hills. From there I'll have them wired to my bank in Nice at a cost of $25 a month. At 10% interest, plus the rate of exchange being 10*ff* to a dollar, I can live in France quite reasonably, albeit frugally.

It's time to tell someone.

"Are you crazy?" My son could not have responded worse. "Going all the way over there? You don't know anybody in France. You don't even know the language. How can you leave your two-year-old granddaughter?" I have to admit, leaving Ashley will be tough. And Howie is right. I don't know the language, but I'll darn well learn it. Reactions all around do not surprise me. Oh, yes, my son, my family and friends are happy for me, but... That's just it, the 'but.' They are afraid for me. I am not. *Au contraire.* After all, the idea did come to me in a lucid moment. Yes, there are terrorist threats and bombings in Paris. But since the

United States Travel   Advisory deems it safe, so be it. I couldn't feel more confident if I had angels on my shoulders guiding me. Maybe I do and nothing can shake them loose. So I go.

Nice

The sailors eventually sleep. The noise diminishes and the horizon begins to glow. Once the sun makes its full, warm appearance I stretch and grin, still floating on last night's visions of the celebration. I'm really here ready to start my new life. But not liking my nocturnal neighbors, I decide to check out of this dismal little place. And after walking around outside, I find the whole neighborhood not to my liking.

Taking my quest further afield on foot to find a more suitable place, it's not long before I arrive at the Hotel Napoleon (an apt French name), with its entrance situated on the corner of two *allées*. This is interesting. And a friendly-looking lobby entices me to further inspect the premises.

Inside, the *concierge* shows me a room at the back that looks adequate: a firm double bed, a large armoire and end table, a lamp, a desk, and enough room to store my soon-to-arrive boxes from home. The best thing of all is its location: one block to the bus, another half block to the *zone piétonne* (Pedestrian Street), and a short walk to the *Promenade des Anglais* and the sea. This could work. But after ten days I take stock. I'm all set at the university, but I have to keep searching for just the right apartment. This time, I'll look from the window seat of an accordion bus that bends in the middle as it turns corners—like an accordion opening up— the back end following right along.

The bus climbs into the *Cimiez* section of Nice, home to the Roman ruins and museums. A very nice residential area from what I'm seeing. Apartments everywhere and each with a view to the shimmering emerald sea. But this section also expands away from the core, the pulse of the city. And with my love for freedom I would have to depend upon transportation each time I'd want to go exploring, to school or for a cup of coffee, to sightsee or people-watch. But as the days wane, my luck continues.

Over on rue Marichal Joffre I finally find the perfect studio apartment, one block from the hotel where I am currently staying. Miraculously, the boxes I sent ahead have found their way to me. I've also enrolled for afternoon classes at the university, and as fate would have it, I have made a genuine friend here. How propitious that on the day after my arrival I should meet Madame Marguerite Kaufmann, an enlightened and lovely French woman who would play an integral part with my assimilation and understanding of the *French,* and myself. My pastor/counselor back home had given me her name, but I never expected that she and I would hit it off so effortlessly. From our first conversation she's treated me with such benevolence, understanding and patience. But most of all, love. We've been telephoning each day, in fact.

How beautifully everything is coming together. A very good omen, I think.

Perfect.

4

W hile I had envisioned living in an architecturally significant, even romantic edifice (And why not dream?) I find my new residence a rather drab and mediocre building. It seemed enough that I was in France, living on the Côte d'Azur. Naïve reasoning reassures me though that I can always move if I should find something more…well, *French.*

The front door to my new apartment opens into one enormous room with sliding glass double doors on the far wall that lead out to a narrow balcony. Near the front door inexpensive-looking artifacts line a set of bookshelves, while a nondescript, upholstered sofa bed accompanied by a single vinyl-seated armchair and a Formica-topped table with four utilitarian chairs tries its best to spruce up the big space. (Right out of *Architectural Digest.*) Still, it all fits nicely and with room to spare. And maybe I can move the table and chairs out onto the balcony for al fresco dining. Traffic noises below, along with my favorite tapes, will accompany my dining. Not fancy, but doable. Yes, I can live with this.

Now, what could be called the kitchen really is a nook with a bar-sized sink. Not four burners—as is the norm—but a two-burner range, a miniscule fridge, and a few skinny cupboards. No gourmet meals prepared in this space. I guess I can stand to lose a little weight. Still, I won't be able to avoid the kitchen entirely. Necessity will force me to use it on occasion. Necessity also demands some groceries. Soon.

Despite the drizzle and predicted showers for the day, and since I am desperate to get food into the apartment, I decide to go grocery shopping anyway. As a prelude to rain, dark clouds have been piling in all morning, but I figure I still have plenty of time and doggedly embrace the challenge. This is, after all, my first attempt at trying to be *French*. So off I go, out into the streets of Nice on my first adventure as an actual resident.

Along my route little neighborhood *marches* dot the street and alleyways. Colorful produce sprawls artfully on tabletops or is stacked neatly in tipped boxes that purposely spill out toward the sidewalk. A glance inside some of the shops shows a smattering of other food staples too. On an earlier perusal of this area I'd noticed two stores that actually sell milk and butter and cheeses. The Galleries Lafayette Department Store (much like our Macys) on Avenue Jean Médecin has a rather gourmet section on its lower level. Farther east about four blocks is the Woolworth-like Prisunic—a vast complex with a wide linoleum stairway that descends to below street level to a market. I choose Prisunic for my grocery shopping debut since its closer to rue Marichal Joffre.

And though I anticipate a simple expedition walking down these barren steps of Prisunic, I'm experiencing something akin to unreality—I am about to shop as an actual resident, not as a tourist searching for souvenirs. Nice is my home now. For however long.

With my head in the clouds and feeling giddy, I grab a cart and proceed to fill it. I need everything. Decadent and exotic merchandise surrounds me, things I cannot buy in the States: creamy chocolate spread (wow!), *confiture de figue* (must be fig jam) and, oh, my goodness! —*the milk cartons are not refrigerated.* Like the proverbial kid in a candy store I mosey down the aisles, anticipating some glutinous eating back at my new apartment and paying little mind to the other shoppers with tote bags over their arms. I continue to thread my way between stacks of merchandises, plucking various items from their shelves and steering my brimming cart to the nearest checkout stand.

To my amazement the clerk hands me several small plastic bags. *What are these? She wants me to bag my own groceries?* I plead timidly, "But these are *très petites.* Unmoved and without so much as a glance my way she points to some larger bags, any of which I can buy for two *francs* each. I buy three. But she's not finished. She rambles something off in French, all the while jabbing the air in the direction behind me. Bordering on panic, I glance in the given direction then back to her. *What is she trying to tell me?* Again, I look over my shoulder. All I see is the produce section. Nothing. I look back at her. Still nothing. But from behind me, whispers of *"Américaine"* have me turning around yet again. Impatient shoppers have since lined up, each one shaking his head. Then, *ah.* Beyond their wagging heads and prominently displayed in the produce section—a sign. In French, naturally.

ALL PRODUCE MUST BE WEIGHED AND MARKED BY THE
ATTENDANT.

Mon Dieu! I rush past the line of grim faces to the produce clerk who
carefully weighs and marks my little treasures. By now a wave of heat has spread
over the back of my neck, and even my ears feel hot. I rush back to the clerk in a
state of sweltering humiliation and toss my remaining groceries—in their *très*
petite bags—onto the counter, which has not stopped moving in my absence. I
search the counter area, but...*where are my other groceries?* My face is pulsing
now with heat and blinking, I imagine, like a neon light: Look! Look! *Américaine!*
The cashier tallies my bill, and finally she looks at me. Totally distraught and not
about to hold up the line a second longer, I press my money into her extended
hand, hoist what few goodies I have, and start for the exit, my eyes fixed straight
ahead. I cannot walk fast enough back up these linoleum steps, thinking how the
smallest things can so quickly shatter a confidence. The closer I get to the doorway
I feel the outside air starting to cool my face. I draw in a slow, steady breath and
try to regain my composure.

Out into the street the first tiny drops tap my nose and cheek. I look up.
Apparently, I misjudged the weather too. Very dark clouds are about to give way. I
hug my *très petite* bags to my chest and dash from the site of my disgrace for
home. I just hope the bags that are getting soaked will hold together.

No such luck. Worse. My bags burst over the counter top, and in the solace of
my kitchen nook I delve into the soggy mess.

No *poulet* (chicken).

No *riz* (rice).

No vegetable oil.

No Swiss cheese or oranges.

Hereafter, I must invest in a large, string-expandable bag and keep my purchases to small amounts at a time. Since that incident I've become very visual and aware. No matter where I happen to be, I watch the actions of people around me before venturing forth. With this insight I feel more at ease and avoid blunders and distressing situations. I'm also picking up words and phrases and bravely using them. I even find the French friendlier and more accepting as I do so.

However, still unnerved by the grocery shopping incident, I decided to wait a couple of days before venturing out to get a phone. To assure that it would go more smoothly I contacted *Mme* Amar, who represented me in the apartment transaction. She graciously arranged everything by telephone, including my new number. All I need to do now is to head over to the phone company with that number. Fortunately, I live downtown and everything is within walking distance.

Inside the spacious telephone office I amble up to the reception area, tear a numbered white slip from a little machine, and settle in with the waiting throng— each one fingering his own little white slip. *Even in France.* Sometime later I hear my number called. I jump up and approach a receptionist. She speaks no English. Again the murmurs—"*Américaine!*" And the heads wag. *Of course, I don't know French yet,* I want to shout, *I've only been in France two weeks. Give me a break.* Then it occurs to me that I am outside the tourist area, mingling with the everyday working folk and should probably know the language. How many tourists seek telephones? *Ah.* But in my head the murmurs crescendo. I glance from one blank face to the next.

"Does anyone here speak English?"

"*Un peu,*" a faint voice responds. I explain my situation to this benevolent stranger, and he plunks me down in front of a clerk who is sitting behind a desk. I give this darling girl my number and my name, which she then punches into a computer. *Voilà!* My address pops right up. Then the query: What color do I want? "Brown, *s'il vous plâit.*" That's that. I say *merci*, give a grateful smile to the non-English-speaking receptionist, and walk out the door with my brand new phone.

Now, until I had purchased food for my cupboard I loved spoiling myself at various neighborhood bistros or *brasseries*. Consequently, this slight indulgence has me arriving home after dark, and so far this hasn't been a problem.

Tonight, having just exited the elevator to my apartment, I stop to locate my key in my purse when the lights go out. I can't see a bloomin' thing. In my panic I realize I haven't memorized the layout of the hallway. How far to my door? I'm clueless but I can't stay here.

With my purse in hand, I stretch out my arms. With baby steps, I feel my way to the wall. Groping along this wall I remind myself to calm down; it's early, someone is bound to come along and rescue me. Sure enough.

From behind me I hear the elevator door open. A wonderful circle of light illumines a sparse area in the hall. A woman steps confidently into that glorious glowing circle and rather intentionally touches the wall. *What is she doing that for?* But here come the hall lights. *You've got to be kidding.* I rush to my door and open it, flip on my apartment light, rush back to the doorway and wait. Just as I predicted. The hall lights blink off. And now that I'm consciously looking I see them—little bulbs glowing orange-like and placed sporadically down the hallway—I reach down and press the one nearest me. The hall lights come back on. *Aha!* They must be conserving energy in this building. I wonder how many other buildings do this. Thank God, my private domain is not under the control of Mitterrand's government. Sometimes now, when I go to check the lobby mailbox in the early evening the lights go out. I still have to feel my way to the closest orange button and maybe, just maybe, I'll make it into the elevator before they go out again. (Thankfully, no one is ever standing next to me when this occurs; they would be surprised at what comes out of my mouth, albeit in English.)

Handling the garbage is something I still need to acquaint myself with, so I am investigating to see what one does with their trash in France. I try to remember what *Mme* Amar had told me that first day, while she was acquainting me with the building and my apartment. There was so much to take in, and with the excitement of having my own place who could remember all such miniscule instruction?

Threading my way now through the building, I faintly recall 'a door to the left of the elevator and stairs that lead to a basement.' And if I remember correctly, inside this door and 'straight ahead on the left, before descending the stairs,' there should be another little door. *Yes. Here it is.* I open it and find what resembles a bank depository. *Odd-looking garbage chute.* But since I'm leaving for Monaco shortly, I probably should take care of my trash now instead of later.

I head back upstairs to grab my two full-to-the-brim bags, then back down the stairs to this door with the depository-looking bin. I step inside the doorway, and as the door is closing behind me I catch it with my foot. As intuition prompts me, and with both arms full, I hug the one bag to my side, reach for the door handle and try to twist it. It doesn't budge. *If this door had closed tight...* Fear shoots through me. I don't even want to wonder. I wedge my foot between the door and the jamb, and slowly I set one of the bags down. With my free hand I reach over and open the *chute de garbage*. With the other hand I push the bulging bag into the chute. *Mon Dieu*! It doesn't fit. I let out a heavy sigh. I have no choice.

I reach in and pull out a sticky carton.

A handful of greasy cans.

Saturated pulps of paper.

I cram them, one by one down the skinny throat of this monster and listen. Each item kinda tumbles down the shaft—my foot still jammed in the door, and my right thigh starting to scream. I dip my fingers then into something squishy, when—*oh, my gawd*—the lights go out. 'Patience, my dear…' The words of my new friend, Marguerite, come to me. Then oh—so calmly—I close—the bag. I step out into the hall and listen for the door to close. I find the wall and slide my slimy hand to the nearest orange button and push the darn thing.

Back inside my apartment I put what is left of my garbage in its rightful place under the diminutive kitchen sink, scrub my hands, and leave for Monaco. It is imperative, however, that I revisit this garbage mystery, since I have no manager or *concierge* in my building. (I do so the next day, in fact.)

I remembered *Mme* Amar having told me about a storeroom in the basement. She had actually taken me there. *How could I have missed that? Aha!* Now I remember. There are two basements.

With my smelly bag I cautiously open my front door (as if no one else has garbage?) and set off to find that mysterious chute. This time I take a flashlight. And there it is. Well, there they are: four garbage pails standing all in a row. I dump my little treasures into one of the bins and return to the elevator just as it is opening. A nice lady stands inside the elevator, obviously coming down to empty her garbage and, would I hold the door for her? *Mais certainment!* We *bonjour* each other, and I ride back up to the fourth floor feeling very wise.

5

My life in Nice is settling into such a comfortable routine, and my apartment is beginning to feel like home. Thanks to the suggestion of a friend back in Laguna I'd brought some personal belongings with me, to assist in my transition and ease any homesickness. A few of my favorite books now perch on my bed stand: *Gift from the Sea*, Stuart Wilde's *Affirmations*, and Shirley MacLaine's *Out on a Limb*. On the bookshelf near the front door I arranged some framed photos of my family, including one of my grand-daughter, Ashley. Jean Claude, my white faux-fur polar bear, who previously was squashed into my suitcase for the trip, is all fluffed up now and stretched out on my sofa. The next thing to do is to make another list. I'm a list maker, I always have been. Lists give me direction, and I knew this would be a life-changing experience and would need to be organized. If I plan to have an adventure here I don't want to stress out about anything. I want all bases covered. So, the personal list and the home list have already been created.

And after my son practically accused me of abandoning my two-year-old granddaughter, it behooves me to make sure I don't neglect her. I've devised a plan for the mailing list of friends and family who expect regular up-to-date information from this nomad. I'll keep them updated with copies of a hand-written letter. I will always address them: 'Dear Ashley' and always end with: 'I love you, Mer Mer' (baby Ashley's word for *Grandmere*). Thank heavens for copy machines, there's one within walking distance. I'll make several copies and send my letters off right away. With an explanation and prior approval, everyone back home (who matters) thinks this arrangement rather quaint.

School has since started. Monday through Friday, from one o'clock to four, I have been studiously attending my university classes. But with mornings free I thought it a fabulous idea to enroll in the *Alliance Française*. It's such a short walk from my apartment I knew I could easily be there from nine o'clock to noon. In addition to teaching French, the *Alliance Française* schools are culture centers for social affairs; French movies are part of the curriculum, and kindred French souls gather for great camaraderie.

In the mornings now, I walk one mile to the *Alliance Française* with a hard-boiled egg and apple. After class, I walk another mile to the university while eating my lunch. In addition to homework, keeping my lists current is keeping me busy at night. I must say I feel rather proud of myself doing everything possible to assimilate into this culture. And I still talk regularly with Marguerite. "Well, my dear," she'll say to me, "how did your day go?"—her usual question. "Everything's going great," I tell her. "I find it so stimulating. Though I like my teacher, I feel so stupid. The French is not coming." Her usual answer? "Patience, my dear"—like a mantra. I see her beatific face always expressing an irrepressible smile. As I talk of the problems that brought me to France, she is helping me to find a seed of significance to this second stage of my life, always reminding me that my new life starts now and each day thereafter is a new beginning.

Nice continues to welcome and embrace me. Although, for the record, I've not been under any illusion that the French would welcome me with open arms. On the contrary. I know their culture to be aloof and proud. Under first impressions I sense them to be tolerant, but in no hurry to be friends with Americans or other expatriates. If they have never lived among us, have never absorbed and accepted our idiosyncratic behaviors, they merely see us as visitors. If these new French acquaintances view me as a tourist, it's up to me then, to expand my horizons and seek outside interests and friends. For the time being, I will quietly immerse myself and embrace their culture. How better to accomplish this than by learning their language.

Once I discovered that a television would hasten my goal, I obtained one the very next day. There is just this one disconcerting aspect of my life, however. I'm not going out on any dates or even enjoying any social interaction with adults. Certainly, Louis Jourdan and I will never cross paths as I schlep my dirty laundry to the nearest *laverie. C'est la vie!* It was bound to be, since most of my time is occupied with school.

"*Bonjour, Marie Cécile.*"

"*Bonjour, Mar-ee-lyn.*"

From the beginning this has been our daily ritual upon entering our classroom.

She requests and we gladly acquiesce. But not to '*Madame*' or '*Professeur.*'

Petite with short cropped, curly black hair, Marie Cécile speaks no English. And we, her students, speak no French. But her friendliness and unorthodox teaching is helping us to break through the French-speaking-only barrier. I'm learning more here than in a typical day in other traditional classrooms I've sat in. She has unorthodox methods, such as when she brought in from her neighborhood *fromagerie* a chunk of goat cheese for us to savor and comment on: the aged versus the new. She has shared with us her favorite shops in the *vieille ville* and introduced us to her favorite gated-restaurant, which has no business sign on its exterior (obviously a secret known only to a special clientele). "If you plan to go there," she instructed, "just knock on the gate and say that Marie Cécile sent you." One evening, a small group of us did go. It worked. In minutes we'd devoured an unforgettable, authentic *Niçoise* meal. And since she lives in the old village, an excursion to her home today will further add to our learning experience, I'm sure.

Directly off a cobblestone *allée,* Marie Cécile pushes open a newly-refurbished wooden door on the face of an unremarkable relic of a building. She leads us in through a windowless vestibule. To my right, a dank and forbidding hallway barely glows from a diminutive light of a shaded and dusty wall sconce. We follow her up a narrowly curved flight of cement steps. So bowed in their middles, I wonder how many centuries of footsteps it has taken to do this. At the top of the stairs she pushes aside a heavily-draped *portiere* and exposes a room that looks more like a cubby. One of many. Through single small windows set deep in their thick walls, filtered light tries to insinuate into each of these dim rooms, but such narrow shafts can hardly brighten up a place. If it wasn't for her bright pillows and wall hangings, these sparsely furnished spaces would feel to me more like tombs. Could I ever live like this? Indeed, this is another world. Another time.

Back in the classroom on a regular day our textbooks are large paperbacks with cartoon characters, which leaves no doubt as to the correct intent of the captioned French word or phrase. They remind me of American comic books. This is obviously French *élémentaire*.

The class is intimate, only fifteen students. Most are younger than my children, and some of us are quickly becoming a family. There is Anna from Denmark—a tall, bronzed 24-year-old who spent the previous summer in Monaco. She speaks a little French but can't read it or write it. And while this new Scandinavian friend is more advanced socially and physically, another new friend, Sophie—with her sheltered upbringing and affluence notwithstanding—is forbidden to go out in her native country unless accompanied by her father or a brother. At age 19, Sophie—a dark-eyed, dark haired sprite—has five older brothers who are living back in Spain; while Ammi, an aloof and married woman in her forties, has come to us from Iran, though she also has family here in Nice. And Omar… The first thing you notice about Omar, our 22-year-old from Egypt, is his flashing black eyes. And I do mean black.

Then we have the American contingent comprised of Vicki, a 20-year-old from Connecticut, who is interested in Amnesty International. Keith, our youngest at 18, is blonde and slim and manages to infect us daily with his enthusiasm and contagious habit of bounding into the classroom raring to go. Dana is also spunky —she's 20 years old, from San Francisco and has come here merely on a lark. Coming from Beverly Hills, California, is petite and married and classic Judith—

formerly a ballerina who wants to pursue her desire to learn French. The eldest student and grandmother at age 55 is me. Together we are a mini United Nations.

Most of my new friends live in rented rooms or private homes or in dorms off campus, so it is at my meager apartment that we occasionally gather after school for a little social time. Occasionally, I'll even pull *une bière* from my fridge. From the school, we walk together the two miles along the sea and stop for soft drinks along the way. As these nine younger students and I connect, I'm quickly adopting the preferred dress code of the day: casual, which means jeans. While I prefer walking boots, occasionally I succumb to wearing tennis shoes. I'm surprised to see Marie Cécile dress so casually, sometimes even wearing jeans. Let's say I expected a more traditional-looking *professeur*. Her equally informal greeting always puts me at ease.

In the classroom she never adopts the same demeanor. At times, she will stand and point to the lessons on the blackboard or white video screen. Other times, she leans against our long table to lecture us on the day's assignment. Often she effortlessly maneuvers her slight frame to the top of our long table—poised in the middle of us, either crossed-legged or with her elbows resting on her upturned knees—to expound on the most interesting subject. Just your run-of-the-mill teacher? Hardly. But then this isn't your run of the mill class. But this is my first experience fraternizing with so many foreign students at one time. So far it's been incredibly exhilarating. Everyone participates in the communal gabfest, and though tongues fly in different languages laughter keeps us grounded in harmony.

So here I am, thrust into a veritable goldmine of diverse thinkers with their strong opinions, passionate philosophies, and non-judgment—a truism of the idiom 'Freedom of Speech.' I feel a profound and awesome sense of well-being in this interaction of young, seeking minds with their dissimilar views on life and culture. We talk openly in our ragtag of languages; we really are as one—united. It's been the closest thing to recapturing my youth. And when the conversations start to elevate, each one with as much hunger to articulate as with a great interest to hear what others have to say, I feel myself pulling back to the edge of their orbit and thinking: If any one of these kids should ever become a leader in their respective country, with their young understanding and tolerant minds, the world will be a better place. I can't believe how much I'm absorbing and accomplishing in such a brief time. I want to understand what exists beyond my comfort zone and not shy away from it. My new young friends are helping with that, as they keep challenging my long-held theories and exercising my tolerance for their differing perspectives. I'm compelled daily to seek more knowledge, expand my thinking, and be more understanding and open to pushing aside even my set goals. Never have I felt so connected to a group of people.

These French days have certainly taken on a languid flow. I savor my mornings, *bonjouring* the proprietor on the corner, as he arranges his produce out on the sidewalk. A friendly nod from the now-familiar *zone piétonne* waiter setting his tables makes me feel welcome. I feel like a natural limb these days within the French body of humanity. Yes, a small semblance of a routine has emerged, and the days seem to be clicking by without worry. Until the letter arrived.

6

S everal weeks into my new idyllic life on the Côte d'Azur I received a letter from my accountant, Jim. He assured me months before I'd left that my financial picture was completely satisfactory for my plans. I would have to pay taxes, of course, but not enough to jeopardize my trip. Now he's telling me that he made an error in his calculations. Instead of the reasonable cushion for overseas expenses, I'm now looking at having to pay twice what he'd calculated. This news couldn't be worse. It's as if a tsunami has engulfed me, and for days I haven't been able to break free. Was I wrong to take this journey? I have been keeping my real estate license current; is this some subconscious net to fall back on? The thought of returning to that hectic pace sends a shiver through me. I am not about to go backwards. I can't. Not now. No, no, no. It's natural to doubt, but I can't let doubt or fear defeat me. A new beginning awaits me here. I'm certain of it. I feel it. And I will wait for it.

Nonetheless, a slight pall lingers in the air. I think I just need to get out of the apartment and breathe.

On various occasions already I've visited the *vieille ville* and strolled down several of its *allées* that converge into open neighborhood squares. But today I turn down a favorite *allée* and follow its familiar meandering path. I come up to the old church I like so much, with its intricately-sculpted facade and elaborately-carved spires that beckon the faithful. It looks out of place couched amid modern, brightly-colored *cafés*, *chocolatiers*, galleries, souvenir shops and bistros. Across the way is a bistro with cozy wrought-iron tables out front. I think one of the tables must have my name engraved on it; it's empty every time I come this way. I walk over and succumb to the chair's silent beckoning: "Marilyn, over here."

The waiter ambles over and quietly, politely takes my order. A *vin sec* to sip, while I watch the people—sparse this time of year. Even the air feels off-season this morning. What little activity I do see bares no feel of urgency, just steady and calm. I pull in a deep breath and let it out nice and slow. I listen to the gurgle from a modest fountain a stone toss away. Clear water cascades uninterrupted—the perfect 'white noise' to center my thoughts. Thoughts that need to be addressed, I guess.

The waiter sets my drink on the table and I thank him. Now then, the letter.

How could Jim have made such a blunder? What if this drastic move wasn't necessary? For a moment, I consider any other move that might've kept me closer to my family. Maybe I should have stayed in Laguna. Could I have eventually made a go of things? Stay on? Persevere? Push through the talk behind my back? Faces flood back to me, and I recall the comments that were made. I remember that this decision was not made in haste; I'd agonized over it. I replay the circumstances that pushed me here. The old feelings move through me, as if it's happening all over again. Do I honestly regret this move? What if Jim's letter is some divine message of a huge mistake I've made? A rush of panic shoots through me and my stomach drops. I slow my breathing, try again to become one with the placid movement around me—the perpetual gurgle of the fountain water, gulls calling to each other in their loops overhead.

I close my eyes.

Images of Anna, Sophie and Omar, Vicki, Keith, Dana and Judith; my amazing teacher, Marie Cécile; my new life mentor, Marguerite—each in their unique way is awakening something in me. *I relish this growth in me, at my age.* And I recall an event many years ago.

I was in my early twenties. I had just moved to Newport Beach, California, and had applied for a job at the City Hall. Within a matter of days, much to my surprise, I discovered a telegram slipped under my front door. A telegram from Boy Scouts of America, New York. An International Boy Scout Jamboree was scheduled in seven months' time, to be held in Corona del Mar, just south of Newport Beach. They were looking for an assistant to the Chief Commissary Officer, burdened with the feeding of the 60,000 hungry boys scheduled to be in attendance for a period of two weeks. An appointment was scheduled for 11 a.m. the following day and, would I be interested? I jumped at this unique opportunity. For the next six months, I worked in a Quonset hut organizing, implementing, interviewing vendors, ordering and tasting all the foods necessary for this massive undertaking. During that time I had the opportunity to meet scout executives from around the world. Most especially, the scout executive from the nearby city of Santa Ana. At the conclusion of the jamboree, again unemployed, Skip Fife, the executive of Orange Empire Council, Boy Scouts of America, approached me and offered me the position of personal secretary and bookkeeper. I had trepidations about the bookkeeping, so I turned to my associate, Iris, the only other woman in our cozy Quonset hut. "Marilyn," she said, "Can you balance your checkbook?" I told her, "Well, of course." So there it was. I went on to my bookkeeping job, which included a weekly payroll.

Opportunities here in France are just as stretching, challenging me and building a confidence I didn't believe I was capable of having. Neither have I experienced such simple gratification before. The people in my life today are oddly aware of what is significant. They are as intent to enjoy living as they are tireless to meet their goals. Like lasers aimed on their targets. So why can't I do the same? I just need to discover my target. And I will. But these people…

I can't get over how intent they've been to pull me into their lives. One day we were introducing ourselves, and the next moment, it was as if we were long-lost relatives. Our paths are crossing for only a brief time, yet we have this sense of grabbing the most of this time together. Not one of us is using anyone because of influence. No one is out to impress with titles or prestige. *Here* is a leveled field, where we each give and take merely of ourselves. And just as they are learning about me, I'm gaining from them and from my teachers and Marguerite a renewed trust in people. And ironically, I owe this profound purity of life to the mire that led me here.

Regrets? None whatsoever. To say I am 'happy' is an understatement. I can honestly look back over the previous couple months and see how I've been embracing each day. Not once—no matter how difficult the adjustment has been so far—have I looked for a way out. This has not been a cake walk, but I haven't collapsed under the challenges. Daily tasks in Nice certainly take much more effort and confidence, of which I'm gathering. Back home such tasks rarely demanded a second thought. But here?

Just using public transportation tests my capabilities. As did having film developed and making long-distance calls from the post office. Oh, and when I went to have my walking boots half-soled I had to use a dictionary. I had to write down every word to explain exactly what I needed. How painfully I persevered through what should've been the simplest communication. I exerted the patience of a saint until the shoemaker and I finally came to an understanding. "*Fait accompli!*" He smiled indulgently. A few days later, behold! —a practically new pair of boots sporting a fine gloss. And since the Place Grimaldi shoemaker is only two blocks from my apartment, I poke my head in his door from time to time, just to *bonjour* him.

No, my decision to move here will not become another failure. This was the right move.

I sigh. Maybe not the best financially, but most assuredly ordained. There has to be a solution to Jim's new findings. I just need to think clearly. In fact, I'll call and ask him to extend my deadline to October. That'll give me eight months to reconsider my situation.

In the meantime, I've got places to see and people to meet and much to absorb.

7

I t takes me exactly ten minutes to walk from my apartment to the

Mediterranean Sea and the Promenade des Anglaise. The Promenade is my retreat,

with its wonderful benches that sprawl sporadically along the expansive concrete

above the rocky seawall. This walk stretches for miles around a half moon. On

foggy mornings I love to sit with my cup of *café*, while a company of seagulls

usually sweep the bit of sky above me. On warm evenings, while the red ball takes

its sweet time dipping into the horizon, I come and sit here and sip a *vin sec*. I

never tire of watching the sea. The southern portion of this promenade merges

right into the old village, the *vieille ville*.

Every European city has their 'old village,' where their unique history stands

preserved from inside ancient walls. It wasn't until the 17th Century before Nice

expanded upward from the walls of its old village. Tucked snug as teeth in the narrow jawline of the Mediterranean coast, quaint hotels have since been rooted in alongside old world cathedrals and other medieval buildings.

But down close to the shore here, inside these old walls, alleyways branch off and climb and wind around every which way, always flanked with high banks of multi-storied structures and lined with warrens of shops and stalls that inhabit *pâtisseries*, *boucheries*, bistros, with sun-drenched patios and tourist-catering souvenir shops.

Also nestled among these antiquities (such as my favorite old church) is an elaborate-canopied opera house. Colorful displays of performances adorn its facade. I love to browse through an open market a short distance from here, along the Cours Saleya, open from early morning until noon. Promptly at noon then, the workers scurry around demolishing tables, cleaning up every last bit of detritus— just in time for waiting residents and tourists to claim their seats at the outdoor cafés. The French love to bask in the sun with their *apéritifs*.

Further south and rising out from a high bluff, an ancient castle overlooks the harbor and appears still to be protecting its domain. Marguerite and I regularly shop at this old village, specifically to visit a *boucherie*. I don't know what fascinates me more, the *boucherie* or Marguerite—the way she can explain to the butcher the exact cut of meat she wants.

Meats hang from the ceiling on long metal hooks. Or they're displayed behind large glass panels. Not at all like our meat counters in America, where butchers pile their cut-and-packaged items on top of each other. This is definitely a butcher shop, and I'm fascinated seeing meats displayed as they are here.

Among the unique fish prevalent in Nice and along the Mediterranean shore is the *truite rouge* (red trout), which I just love. And flowers—just as important to the European meal as in America. Banks and banks of them stacked in front of the little shops, so it's nearly impossible to leave without one small bouquet. Marguerite is always buying flowers, as they are an expression of beauty and add to the pleasure of dining. A table bouquet certainly makes me want to take my time to enjoy my meal, let it settle and savor the moment. Meals, I'm learning, are meant to tend to the mental and emotional health, not merely to tickle the taste buds and satisfy a groaning stomach.

The old village…it's my favorite place to go.

Nice sprawls upward directly from the sea into its surrounding hills. Despite its modern thoroughfares and eclectic architecture, everything is steeped in antiquity. I don't find it necessarily beautiful or charming, but I can certainly understand why it's become a vacation haven for those fortunate or wealthy enough to enjoy it. The climate and its proximity to Italy, Monaco, and Cannes, is ideal. Not to mention all the picturesque coves, ancient villages perched on nearby hilltops, and exclusive enclaves along the shoreline. Nice is the heart of the Riviera, distinctly, the French Riviera. Its diverse history by former rulers makes it an interesting mélange of characterization—and not necessarily French.

I delved further into its fascinating history: formerly ruled by Sardinia and Savoy and, more recently, by Italy, Nice has only been a part of France since 1860. Yet a Mediterranean flavor is evident in its *Niçoise* food, the residents' more swarthy complexions, and a more casual attitude and dress. Thanks to a vacationing British doctor and novelist, in 1763 this miles-long paradise by the sea would become the prime vacation spot for sun-deprived Brits. I would have thought that by enduring the long journey from England it would have made the coastal nirvana even more inviting. But it wasn't for another 57 years, in 1830—

after the British had built the *Promenade des Anglais* alongside the *Baie des Anges* (Bay of Angels)—when they actually descended on Nice as a winter watering hole. By then, hordes of wealthy English strolled *en mass* along the tranquil sea. Even today mothers are out alongside me pushing their strollers, and cyclists ride past us. And there are plenty of dog walkers and skaters to observe and *bonjour*. I am far from being alone. Everyone comes out to enjoy the sun-splashed *promenade*.

Another slice of historical Nice is the little-known Paillon River. I'd heard rumors and wondered whatever happened to it. I've since discovered that in another time long, long ago, it used to flow right through Nice on its way to the Mediterranean Sea. But it has since been covered over. I wasn't aware of this before, but today it's flowing beneath Nice. Here I've been walking back and forth over the Paillon River and didn't know it.

In the 1500s, laundresses dared to ply their trade along its treacherous shores. Over time, the hazards and consequences of daily exposure to the open and dangerous waters had taken their toll. 300 years later, in the 1830s, the Paillon vanished altogether— forever exiled beneath the boulevards and parks of Nice— including the extraordinary Espace Messena. I certainly don't have to look far or dig deep to discover intriguing bits of history. It's everywhere I turn. And beneath my feet too, apparently.

In these first couple of months it's as if Nice could be any large city. But the instant spring arrives, in comes the glorious weather and the tourists. How fortunate that I'm able to live on this playground for the rich and famous, yet I am neither. But I do like to have fun and other destinations beckon.

There are places in and around Nice and possibly to adjoining countries I want to explore during school breaks. So I'm adding the travel list. I find myself living two lives here. While the serious me pursues learning and understanding the French, the more spirited me continues to revel in *touristing* about. So my first destination will be to Geneva, a French-speaking country. And with a little rationalization, I figure I can justify the expense—thoughts of Jim's letter always at the back of my mind, prodding me to be frugal. I'll chalk this trip up to 'continuing education,' take the night train going and the day train coming back, for diversity. Easy access to surrounding countries is one of the perks of living in Europe.

The afternoon for my first out-of-Nice solo excursion is here. After bouncing along one mile with a packed duffle bag slung over my shoulder, I arrive at the railway station. Four o'clock sharp, but where's my train? The sign says 4:00 departure for Geneva. Okay, I'm good, but I still don't see my train. *Oh, my gawd.* Daylight Saving Time. I could kick myself. What a way to start. The bus left one hour ago.

I tote my heavy heart over to the ticket agent, and after a lot of back-and-forth in my mangled French, he and I think it best if I come back tomorrow afternoon, rather than try for a later train today. What a dismal beginning.

It's the next day, and here I am back at the train station, where my orientation in a communal sleeping compartment is about to begin. I'm excited. Three bunks on one side of my compartment and three on the other side. At least I can draw a curtain for privacy.

Being the first of the cabin mates to arrive, I pick a lower right bunk, stretch out in my limited space and wonder who my traveling companions will be. Who knows? I guess I'll find out soon enough. A feeling of elation envelops me. It usually does whenever I embark on a new adventure.

Just as I settle in for a good read, anticipating an uneventful trip to Geneva, *bam!* —the door to my compartment bursts open, and in storms what sounds like an army. Not an army though, only five young men wearing navy blue blazers. *School boys?* They tear their ties from around their necks and abandon them to wherever the straps of silk happen to fall. Off come their navy blue jackets—each emblazoned with a gold emblem—and thrown without ceremony over the sides of the bunks. I'm invisible at this point; they're much too caught up haggling and jostling each other for their respective berths.

Two of the five clamor up the ladders to the top bunk, toe off their shoes and watch them thud to the floor. The lankiest of the boys on the lower bunk pulls a paper bag from his backpack and waves it in the air, like it's a French flag on VE Day. The two left standing dive for it. One boy leaps from the top bunk, while the other one leans down from his perch for a determined swipe. They can't be more than sixteen, seventeen.

The compartment door is still wide open, and I'm surprised to see a pleasant-looking conductor in the doorway. He pokes his head inside the compartment, looks at me, looks around at the raucity and rolls his eyes. "*Ca va bien?*" he asks me. Not sure everything *is* all right, I can only smile before he slides the door shut —abandoning me to my fate, I'm thinking. Moments later the door slides open, and the conductor informs me of an empty berth top in another compartment a few doors down. There is one drawback, however. The elderly man in the adjoining birth snores loudly. So here it is: a sleepless night on a top bunk with a snoring roommate or this lower bunk in a compartment full of exuberant youth on spring break. The snoring won't bother me as much as climbing a ladder to the claustrophobic heights of a top bunk. Here in my lower booth, if worse comes to worse, I can easily leave. I choose to be with the boys, thinking this might be a little more interesting.

The conductor apologizes, and I settle in feeling like a den mother to my traveling buddies. So much for a quiet read.

With my duffle bag scrunched against the wall on my right side, I contemplate my trip to Geneva, a week in a quaint hotel, a cruise on Lake Geneva and lots of exploring. Casually perusing one of the brochures I'd brought with me, I wonder more what Geneva has to offer these boys—other than the Palais des Nations—when one of them gets my attention. Naturally, my curiosity is aroused.

One by one, the boys become more talkative and enlighten me further. Maybe they feel empowered after having sipped whatever is in that rumpled paper bag. Come to find out, they are Americans attending a private school in Majorca.

The boy with the crumpled paper bag pulls out the mysterious bottle and offers me some Scotch. It's a polite enough gesture, albeit, out of a crumpled paper bag. But picture this, sipping Scotch with underage school boys in a private train compartment. I decline, though we do exchange some light repartee before I excuse myself and pull the curtain closed. I think maybe, just maybe, I might eventually get some sleep. It's beginning to appear that nearly all my social contacts these days are with students. But at this very minute—and so reminiscent of the Orient Express with our lighted compartment, the black night outside the window, the gentle swaying of the train—I wonder, where is the classic handsome stranger?

I take the small tape player/radio I brought with me from the states and wedge the earphones into my ears. Mellow notes of Henry Mancini engulf me, while the party outside my curtain rages on.

In the morning I pull my curtain open and can't believe my eyes. I slip the earphones out and murmur, "Thank you, thank you." My compartment looks like the aftermath of a war zone, and thankfully I managed somehow to sleep through the battle.

Bodies drape across bunks in various stages of undress. Legs and arms dangle over the sides of mattresses. Spittle dribbles from the mouth of one young man, who hangs precariously over the edge of his upper mattress. I resist my motherly instinct to adjust him to a more comfortable position, even to wipe the spittle from his cheek. Tilted bottles, empty food cans, and wadded wrappers lie about the compartment like fallout from an explosion. Ties, socks and shirts drape from the ladder rungs. How apropos, that my friendly little conductor should slide the compartment door open and peek inside. My mouth still dropped, he stares now with open mouth surveying the scene. We look at each other and he just shakes his head. *Poor babies*. Geneva happens to be the end of the line and, I'm not so sure after gauging this disaster, the end of their spring break too. (As for me, my luck will turn, as my company on the Geneva trip will not necessarily end with these boys from Majorca.)

Following an exceptionally good dinner at the hotel in Geneva, enjoying my cup of coffee and contemplating how the stars are in alignment, a handsome older man approaches my table. "May I join you?" he asks. Well, since he speaks English I accept. It also helps hearing that he's the president of a major airline in the United States. He's here on business, which I'm sure does not include a dalliance with a fugitive from the states on leave of her senses. But the evening is still young, as am I, and the night life beckons. With delight, I take advantage of his hospitality and leave our restaurant to tour the back streets and cafés in Geneva's *vieille ville*. Since my social life in Nice has been bereft of men, this is indeed a rare treat feeling somewhat pursued and attended to. Without this companion there are places on this walk that surely would be impenetrable. And as he also speaks French, this trip to Geneva (chalked up to 'continuing education') is proving to be all the more successful.

Geneva is but a memory as I unlock my apartment door and hear the phone ringing. It's Vicki. She and Dana are leaving tomorrow for a week in Florence and, do I wish to go? I'm tired and inclined to say no, but I can't help pondering the wisdom of another trip. Will I get another opportunity? Yet how do I justify a trip to an Italian-speaking country? No answer, but I'm not about to ask myself twice. I might not like the answer.

The three of us buy second-class tickets, board the train and walk to the rear of the car. We see all the empty seats and can't believe our luck. Of course, we pick the best spots, make ourselves comfortable, and thoroughly enjoy the miles and miles of countryside. Not once do we give a second thought to our luxurious seats. As we near our destination a conductor approaches me.

"*Vos billets, s'il vous plait,*" he says. I proudly hand him my ticket and smile, like everything sure is right with the world. "*N'est-ce pas?*" He raises his eyebrows and asks for more *francs*. More? My smile vanishes. I also hear "*premier.*" This can't be good. I look at my friends. Here we've been feeling quite spoiled in this hiatus from reality. *Mon Dieu!*

With our spending money now unfortunately depleted by those plush seats, we have no choice but to stay in a youth hostel in Florence, where we're about to sleep on metal cots and share a communal bath with two other girls. This is 'five girls to a room.' Portable closets house our clothes, while we tuck our duffel bags under our beds. *Another den mother experience.*

We set out eagerly this morning to explore the 'Jewel of the Renaissance.' For starters, a view to the panorama of Florence is in order, so off we rush to the Duomo.

Inside we climb a precarious, circuitous route to the top. 463 steps inside a multi-frescoed dome—each adorned with Giorgio Vasari's renditions of the Last Judgment. Even more spectacular, from the very top of the Duomo all of Florence spreads out below me. Compacted antiquity lies calmingly quiet. Only the air whistles past my ears. What a travesty— such good fortune to walk among all this unparalleled beauty and only a miniscule of time to absorb it.

Reluctantly, we descend the steps. *Going down is so much easier.* Rushing off to the Uffizi, we dash from one painting to the next, upstairs and down, all the while face to face with these masterpieces. I try to visualize de Vinci, Botticelli, and Michelangelo out and about in these parts. And then I walk up to Michelangelo's *David.* His finite contours. His exquisite detail. My mind swells but ceases to comprehend its magnificence. What threads of genius wound throughout Italy in his day!

We stand in line to visit the Pitti Palace. And of course, we have to see the Ponti Vecchio with all its shops, and where, in the middle of the bridge, three archways make a wonderful breezeway for us to sit a spell and enjoy the atmosphere. With my love of history, the Ponti Vecchio intrigues me.

This is the site of the first Florentine gold sellers, the first bridge to cross the Arno until 1218. After the flood of 1345 the bridge was rebuilt. "During WWII, it was the only bridge across the Arno that the fleeing Germans did not destroy" [and] "on November 4, 1966, the bridge miraculously withstood the tremendous weight of water and silt, when the Arno once again burst its banks." [1] Some of these shops are ancient. And while we aren't buying any gold today, for a bargain price on the other side of the river I purchase a peach colored, sleeveless silk blouse, delicately beaded with miniature pearls. *Gorgeous.* But now it is time to find a restroom, which is a lowlight of Florence.

Restrooms in Europe are a subject unto themselves. But such a one actually consisted of a three-sided cubicle and a trough with two indentations in the cement floor—obviously directing me, the desperate visitor, how to adequately spread my feet while squatting. Especially unnerving is their unisex compartments with no seats on the toilets. Said toilets perch flush against a urinal with faulty locks on the doors. I pass up two or three, but…well, one does have to go.

Before we know it our week is over.

Back at the hostel I go to the communal armoire to retrieve my new blouse. It's gone! As are the two girls who shared our humble lodgings. I wasted no time in letting the proprietor know. She offers mere condolences and assures me that nothing can be done. I guess it could be worse. Those girls could have taken everything. *C'est la vie.*

---

[1] Quote taken from: http://www.visitflorence.com/florence-monuments/ponte-vecchio.html

8

After my excursion to Florence its 'back to my routine,' which includes Saturdays with my dear friend and mentor, Marguerite. And this just happens to be Saturday.

In front of the Espace Messena plaza—its fountains jetting like geysers into the sky—stands Marguerite, smiling and waving from under the spray. My heart leaps with fondness, the way her hat perches squarely on her head. This is our day to explore. We kiss each other on both cheeks (typical French greeting) and hike a short distance to a massive terminal.

Like ranks of caterpillars, busses line up in front of their respective destination signs. The choice of exotic places is ours: Cannes, Antibes, Villefranche, St. Jean Cap Ferrat, Beaulieu, St.-Paul-de-Vence, Grasse, Monaco or even Ventimiglia, Italy. Sometimes we pick our locale on a whim. One previous

Saturday morning we'd met at the usual place and got on the bus, but she wouldn't tell me our destination. After ten minutes, we embarked at—of all places—the Nice Harbor. I couldn't miss seeing the ship anchored right in front of us. My dear friend was surprising me with tickets to Corsica. So it was we spent one glorious day visiting the birthplace of Napoleon. Today we've planned for Eze, and I feel quite carefree. Since Marguerite knows the area well (she's lived in Nice four years now), it is me the joyful tourist she wants to please as my guide.

The bus hums along the *Moyenne Corniche,* a middle road halfway up the mountain range that leads to centuries-old villages cleaved from their rocky precipices. Far below me, miniature-looking yachts cut the surface of a vast sparkling playground, tails of white trail behind them. How pristine the sea is. How beautiful the view from here. I think of Grace Kelly and Cary Grant on their way to Monte Carlo, zipping along in a convertible on this very *corniche*, most likely. So this is what it was like. No wonder they fell in love. Colorful villas hug the rugged coastline, most with terraces that tempt some *al fresco* dining under a diminishing sun. This has to be one of the most romantic places on earth.

Our bus arrives, and Marguerite and I disembark into a chilling breeze. My hands take refuge in my jacket pockets. I should have expected a coastal nip in the air. But it's nothing that some trekking up this last slope won't cure, get my blood moving and warming me up.

At the top, a massive stone entrance welcomes us. We pass through its impressive gate and continue along narrow walkways—each one laden with smooth rosy brick and bordered with earthy-colored cobblestone. There is no main thoroughfare here, just narrow walkways that trail like veins in the body of this old world habitation.

We continue upward, interrupted at intervals by a series of steps, and the brick rolling ever out before us like a red carpet. There are several walkways to choose from, as each one meanders off in its own direction. *I think of the different directions I've taken because of someone else's dream. Or the path I took early on with Johnny and how it eventually led us in separate directions.* It's easy to imagine another time, another people along this roaming maze of structures. *We each must find our true path, the path we are meant to travel. Maybe it takes getting lost to appreciate the way that is predestined. Maybe getting lost is part of that predestination—and the heartaches along the way. Will I discover this new life I'm in search of?* My heart is thumping. I feel the strain in my ankles; nothing is level in Eze; it all slopes.

Shouldering me on the path are these antiquated structures with tall rock fronts and facades, and heavy wooden doors set in high cement archways. Now and then, an ornamental wrought-iron placard hanger holding an eye-catching sign —a symbol that clearly communicates what the proprietor is selling—and the name of the shop underneath. Dark wooden shutters complement window openings in their cream-colored stone fronts. We're never walking a straight path with all these curves and corners of buildings splicing into the path's line of vision. It's a bit intoxicating.

We pass several shops whose openings, like mouths to caves, beckon us inside. To appease our curiosity, Marguerite and I slip inside one dimly-lit interior. Amid some exquisite art and handcrafted treasures integral to this area, I can't resist a carved rooster. The rooster is to France what the eagle is to America, I am told.

Continuing with our exploration outside, I notice various residents peering out at us from behind their tiny grill-covered windows. From one opening wafts the most alluring scent of…I breathe in deeply…g*arlic.* We're famished.

Inside the little restaurant the warmth blankets us as we nestle in. After enjoying our fill of *coq au vin,* accompanied by some mellow red wine, we linger over a red checkered tablecloth and sop up the last soggy bites of a baguette. With our appetites sated we're back on the path again, as I savor each step back into ancient history.

"Do you feel like hiking a little?" says Marguerite. I look at her. Shorter than me and 73 years old to my 55, where can she go that I can't? Besides, I've got my comfortable walking boots on.

"Sure," I say rather smugly, "lead the way." We retrace our steps back out of the village and back through the stone entrance. I expect she's heading left down the path we came up on, but instead she veers right toward the sea.

"Follow me." She forges on as if the way is clearly laid out. Then this sprite of a woman has the temerity to say, "Watch your step." Humph. If she can do it, I certainly can. I think. One step at a time. So I follow. Naturally.

Marguerite has been a godsend. I don't know what I would have done so far without her spiritual guidance. She doesn't validate the negativity I'm sorting through, nor does she allow me to wallow. She has this way of putting all the influence from my divulgences of the past into pliable perspective. Nothing riles her, nothing surprises her. She understands humanity. And so she's been helping me to release and forgive and…well, I'm still working on forgetting what lies behind. I'm getting there with her help. She extols me to realize the potential within me that knows no limit. Only I can impose them. Further, I must experience life without fear: fear of failure, fear of success, fear of the future. Nonjudgmental love permeates our time together. A soul mother to me—this petite-but-wise woman whose round, sweet face belies a strong and sometimes feisty nature. It feels as natural to acquiesce to her kind and loving mentorship as it is traipsing down this God-forsaken path.

Across overgrown foliage, Marguerite continues on and over an embankment and...*where is she going?*

I look over the side of the cliff. I no longer see any trail. Still she charges on and down. *Uh-uh, not this kid. No way.* Instantly, I'm back at the high Sierras above Lake Tahoe, the largest Alpine lake in North America. A friend and I are standing at the very top of a ski run. Frozen with fear, I stare down at the miniscule lake at the bottom. "I can't ski down that!" But my friend assures me, "Yes, you can. Just take it one mogul at a time." And with a *whoosh* he's in front of me skiing backwards. Not giving me a second to think, he takes my hand and we're off. I'm taking the Black Diamond trail one mogul at a time, miraculously following him and experiencing the best skiing of my life. "Follow me," says Marguerite, forging on as if the way is clearly laid out.

Zig-zagging like a mountain goat down the side of the cliff I feel my heart thumping. I look up to see where we just were. A boulder blocks the view to the top. *How on earth did she find this trail?*

I'm huffing now and wheezing and half skidding down on my backside. My inadequacy at this sport will be evident tomorrow, or longer, when I nurture my bruised and battered body. *Is there is a cardiologist on call?* The sum of my climbing experiences has only been the 12,000-foot Mt. Tallac at Lake Tahoe, and even that started at a small lake at 6000 feet elevation. The other experience had me negotiating merely a short circuitous trail to our beach in Laguna. We round another patch of shrubs when directly at eye level, a narrow two-lane highway cuts in front of us—and the breath-taking turquoise sea just beyond it. After 60 minutes of plummeting not one word passed between us. Breathing was difficult enough.

At the bottom here (I assume it's the bottom) the ground is slightly level. Yes, we've made it to the *Basse Corniche*, a lower highway that borders the coastline. And here's the tiny hamlet of Eze *sur Mer*. We have actually come down from Eze to Eze-*Bord-de-Mer*.

Marguerite stops.

Thank you, God. I bend over to catch my breath.

She turns to me, her face lit up with a self-satisfied impish grin.

"Wow!" I say. I barely muster the strength for the last few yards to the tiny covered bus stop.

Two exhausted travelers now, we board the next bus and head for home, just as the sun is setting. I discovered later through research that there actually was a trail, exactly where we were zig-zagging down the mountainside. More of a hidden path. It was named Sentier Frederic Nietzsche after the German philosopher, who was renowned for walking up the path instead of down. The arduous trek had left him dizzy, but it inspired the third part of his well-known "Thus Spake Zarathustra," published in the 19th century. While Nietzsche is one of the most influential philosophers even today, in his own lifetime he was not so persuasive. He first visited the Riviera in December of 1883 and penned these words: "Here I grow on the sun as the plants grow there. This splendid plentitude of light has on me a miraculous action."

Thank goodness today is Sunday. I've budged only once from my bed, and that only to answer the phone. It seems my previous day's guide was concerned about my welfare. I must confess to a slight case of jealousy when told she was feeling '*merveilleuse!*'

In the subsequent weeks since my hike, I've been experiencing something akin to a re-coming of age. Somewhat different from when I was in my teens.

Back then I was just setting out into the world, discovering marriage and child rearing, too preoccupied and untrained to notice the years silently filing past me, until I turned around one day and had to look hard at being a middle-aged divorcee, rethinking my life's purpose. 55 years old, and here I am setting out again. I'm more attentive now to the subtle, unrelenting nature of time. I'm wary now too, of wasting or misusing time.

Back then I didn't have a plan really. This time around I'm giving serious thought to what I want to do. My hunger to learn is stronger today than it was in my youth; though this new education is much more revelatory to who I am becoming and to where I may be heading. And though I'm the new kid on the block again, I'm greatly attuned to friendship this time around.

I'm back walking the halls of a school, carrying my lunch, checking out my peers, looking up to a teacher. I have somehow regained my confidence. This is definitely an older me growing up again and, it seems, for the first time.

As for the other things that followed me on this trip? Underneath a fine layer of fresh healing old wounds occasionally still throb. But I do feel myself blossoming into a happier, more confident person, thanks in most part to Marguerite.

9

O n my walks to and from the university I revel in the changing of the season. I look forward to the two-mile trip along the *Promenade des Anglais*— relentless waves crashing over the rocky beach and breakwater. So far this school year the view has changed from an angled sun mirroring a blinding glint off the water, to cumulus clouds roiling over an undulating cerulean sea, to murky and turbulent burnt-umber waters—and me sloshing along under the dome of my umbrella. But all too soon tiny buds are appearing in the abundant promenade flower beds. It's all this early warmth. New green dots the naked limbs of plane trees that border the boulevards in bulk. Lots of geraniums suddenly sporting tight, colored buds will soon be spilling over their boxes. Each sight is claiming its place in the landscape of the living and inspiring new life in me, as well. I can hardly believe this could be spring already.

It's busier along the *promenade* today, now that those who've been hibernating are venturing out, sans their winter wraps and soaking in the sun. Stale winter air finds release, as apartment dwellers open their windows and head outdoors for their long-held habit of sipping a *café au lait*. It's a glorious time for me, being a part of all this synergism, this influx of humanity, as we embrace together the presence of promise. There is still so much more to be experienced here.

One evening, I happened to be having an early dinner in the old village and planning an itinerary for my brother's visit, when a statuesque blond approached the table directly next to mine. I couldn't help but notice her long flowing hair, how it framed her attractively-sculpted face. She was dressed casually enough, a cozy scarf wound around her neck.

Nonchalantly then, she draped her long coat over the back of her chair. There was a definite aura of confidence about her, and I figured she was someone of importance.

The waiter came and took her order of wine.

From her briefcase on the floor between our chairs she lifted out a folder and laid it open on the table in front of her. My curiosity got the better of me, as I glanced at the large, worn sheets of music and words. Not a score for piano or an ensemble, I decided she must be a singer.

"*Excusez-moi.*"

"Yes," she said, "I speak English." I couldn't fool anyone at this point but was relieved she spoke English. In fact, though she is British, she'd studied voice in the United States, in New York.

We chatted for quite a while, as she explained how she'd come to Nice specifically to sing at the opera. *Wow!* —an opera singer singing a little known work of Mozart: "La Finta Giardiniera." I had seen Mozart's "Magic Flute" and loved his Eine Kleine Nachtmusik and others of his works.

While my new friend had a presence about her, she didn't act the diva. On the contrary. She seemed so down to earth I just assumed she was part of a chorus or was playing a minor part. Enthralling. We spent the better part of an hour sharing our stories. She also asked for my address, to send me two tickets to one of her performances. At the time, I didn't pin too much hope on the promise, but a few weeks later two tickets were in my mail. What great timing! Vance will be so surprised with tickets to the opera.

The taxi turns down rue St. Francois-de-Paule in the old village, two blocks up from the sea, and pulls up in front of the old Nice Opera House. I remember gazing at the facade of the opera house some weeks back, wondering if I would be so fortunate. *Here I am.*

A distinguished looking usher greets Vance and me and leads us inside down a narrow and carpeted aisle to our plush seats. I feel so elegant, and I couldn't have asked for a more attractive date. Vance's six-foot frame, his thick brown hair graying at the temples, and an evening scarf around his neck (that insinuates a dapper gent) is an impressive package. And most assuredly a correct assumption.

The seating is limited, but the house is grand and glorious with an ornate, soaring ceiling. Ethereally quiet. I look around and imagine earlier, more illustrious visitors, in their foppish head coverings and brocade and satin finery, who once trod this same carpeted path and sat in these same chairs. Another step back in time. Silently, I thank my new friend for her benevolence, further adding

to my France experience. It comes as no surprise to be seated just five rows from

the front. I can actually see the naps in the velvet stage curtains.

The lights dim.

The curtains part.

Actors descend one by one onto the stage. *Where is she?* After several scenes

I still haven't spotted my friend.

"Maybe she isn't performing tonight," I whisper to Vance. "There are

matinees."

"I don't think she would have given you tickets on a night she wasn't

performing." *This is true.* Nevertheless, the opera is enchanting.

At the end, the entire cast performs a rousing choral rendition. When the lead

removes his cap a cascade of blond hair is loosed. *What is this?* Mozart's star—my

friend, Sandrina—the countess, disguised as the gardener. My heroine bows, and I

applaud with pleasure.

My brother stays with me a couple days more before my life returns to

normal. Which means school and any sightseeing I can squeeze in. Like an

invitation from my classmate, Judith, to accompany her to the Princess Grace

Theatre in Monaco, for an Easter performance of "Rolande" by the London Ballet.

From the states, and for just such an occasion, I brought with me a pale-beige

linen suit with a short-cropped jacket and slightly-full skirt. I'll combine it with a

taupe, silk blouse. Beige shoes and purse compliment my reddish-brown hair and

complete the image. A welcome change from my rather pedestrian school attire, I

feel like I look pretty good and adequately dressed for the occasion. No, that's incorrect. I'm giddy with excitement, getting dressed up and going to the theater in Monte Carlo.

It's a typically brilliant day, as Judith and I catch the bus and head for Monte Carlo, a district of Monaco. The world was to be instantly cognizant of the tiny Principaute de Monaco the moment Grace Kelly married Prince Rainier, thus having saved the Grimaldi Throne that year, in 1956. I am as curious as anyone to visit this tiny royal enclave. Adjacent to the theatre is the casino, where *Chemin de fer*, `blackjack, roulette and other exotic gambling caters to a formally clad clientele. But this is not our destination tonight.

The performance was lovely, and to top it off we dined *al fresco* in Monte Carlo under a moonlit sky. Across the boulevard, we had coffee at the Hotel de Ville. The entire night was magical, one this Nebraska-born girl will never forget. To witness the London ballet in Monaco so soon after attending a Mozart opera in Nice…yes, spring on the Riviera is turning into quite a memorable time. Plus, a three-day weekend in April, Judith and I have decided to rent a car and drive to the Provence, visit Aix en Provence, and then on to Avignon to see the colossal Pont du Gard. (It is recorded that a thousand men under the supervision of Rome spent five years of their lives laying the back-breaking stone it took to create this 3-level bridge. 900 feet long, 160 feet high and 8 1/2 feet wide, the Pont du Gard weighs 50,000 tons, equivalent to the Eiffel Tower.)

From the air, the Pont du Gard looks like a white, stone film strip that splices through the river into both bushy banks. Six wide arches dip their legs into the Gard River, while a walkway stretches across the length of the bridge. From up here, eleven more arches of magnificent white stone slabs rise above our heads.

Above these arches a line of much smaller arches, with yet another walkway above them. The view from there holds all of the known world in every direction.

We make our way down to the base of the bridge, next to one of the legs of these 1st Century AD arches. I am both dwarfed and awed by something so magnificent and ahead of its time.

From here we press on to explore the Roman ruins of Arles and picnic outside the walled Aigne des Meurtes. To milk our weekend we return the long way home along the coast, where towns nestle in pockets that cling to the seashore. The beauty and diversity here has me wishing I'd brought along paints and canvas, as well as the talent to create something with them.

The trip was pleasurable and enlightening and all too short, but a desire to move on is absorbing me. I've been happy and sated, but a complacency is settling in. Boredom. A familiar sign that I've learned all there is to learn from an experience. It's time to move on. Besides, I didn't come here solely to sightsee. I'm restless. I need something more tangible.

It's almost May already. Time to seriously contemplate a move. Maybe to Paris and attend the Sorbonne. Now that is a challenge I can embrace. But am I ready for Paris? What about Polly? My daughter is hoping to spend the month of August with me here. But Nice really is basically just another large French city: Roman ruins, culture center of the Acropolis, Opera, miles of breathtaking shoreline, old village. I've explored and re-explored the villages and absorbed their never-tiring history and charm. I've visited and revisited the galleries and museums. Even the Picasso Museum in nearby Antibes. Nice is not Paris, and this wholly enjoyable life here is certainly not the sum of what I had escaped to.

Perhaps, I've outgrown Nice. As I have embarked on each journey so far, I see how it's been adding to my destiny. The farther along I progress here, those negative events from my past are becoming distant shadows. The progression is teaching me to trust, not ignore, the stirrings in my heart. I must experience the truth of what I'm feeling.

It's settled. I'm moving to Paris. But there is work to be done.

I enrolled for the summer session at the university in Nice and sent a letter off to the Sorbonne requesting to attend their school in the fall. By the end of May, I finished out my studies at the university and concluded my Alliance Francaise classes. New excitement is taking hold of me, with packing my things for the move and planning for my daughter's first trip to Europe. Polly and I will rent a car, drive to Salzburg to attend the Mozart Festival and do some sight-seeing. Then on to Paris. Still, another situation has presented itself.

July is on the horizon, signaling the end of my six months. Some serious thinking needs to be done if I'm going to renew my visa. I realize that six months was an arbitrary time and has passed all too quickly. Life has been so good. With my schooling, blossoming friendships, and lack of financial stress I see no reason to not renew my visa. I just won't set a deadline this time. Let the seasons come. But herein is my challenge, no consulate exists in Nice. And it turns out, I have to pay a visit to the local gendarmes to accomplish this feat. The police station. *Really, a visit to the police?* I hope I have all the necessary information and papers for this appointment.

I woke early, since the station is way over in the old village, and I want to stop for *café* and a croissant. The morning air is sublimely fresh, and there is barely a sound outside. Just your typical shop owner hosing down his part of the sidewalk. And besides one lonesome call of a seagull, it's just me and my *café au lait.*

Continuing on my mission and mentally preparing myself for whatever comes today, I arrive at the veritable hole in the wall that is the station.

Inside, a handful of officers loll about chit-chatting and laughing. In an effort to right himself, one officer nearly falls off his chair. I stifle a laugh amid guffaws from his associates. Hard to believe I'm in a police station, the place feels so relaxed and friendly. And in minutes, as my French proved adequate enough to present my request, I am now set for six more months. Mission accomplished. So simple.

10

S ummer classes at the university are proving challenging this time around. I'm certainly more focused, and the studies are definitely rewarding and much more stimulating. Maybe it's my older frame of mind reentering this bastion of knowledge. Plus, a whole new set of students have just entered my life. It's like starting over again but with some experience behind me now.

I've learned the rudimentary elements of the French language and find it easier to understand now. Speaking French still remains a conscious effort, but this doesn't surprise me. Unless a person has an affinity for languages, younger people just have an easier time picking up a second and third language. But this isn't all.

My earlier, younger classmates have since concluded their studies and gone home. Some, like Vicki, promise to keep in touch. My classes are larger this time, less intimate and as many as 30 or so students. We take our preferred seats amid the tiered seating in what looks more like an arena. We also are expected to act out our assignments on the stage. I find this style more difficult and less personal than the cozy days with Marie Cécile, who used to sit among us in class like a proverbial mother hen; and we, her little chicks, would stroll to and from school together. These new students seem older—college students taking a summer course to speed through their prerequisites, or teachers continuing their education to keep up with ever-increasing learning tools and methods. And there are some like me, who simply want to improve their proficiency in French. I have a feeling that my future here will prove to be far more challenging.

Though I did like school back in the day, I wouldn't go so far as to say that I am scholastically driven. High school had segued directly into marriage and motherhood, and I was solely devoted to Johnny and the children and, later on, to work outside our home. This second half of my life will require the use of a whole new set of emotional and intellectual muscles and skills.

Though I'm not the naïve Marilyn I was when my children were little, I do remember at the time, feeling a timid yearning to expand. But I had no idea of who I was back then or what kind of potential I had. Not a clue. So, this semester I need to seriously rethink my future livelihood. Is real estate a thing to fall back on? Do I want to spend the rest of my days in a constant state of pressure, making fast sales and hoping I'll juggle it all much better than I did before? There is much to work through and learn just by being here.

I think the French have much to teach me. They certainly live healthier. They know how to relax and enjoy life, move at a slower pace. I'm discovering through their lead what really matters, and am challenged to reconsider my future. And though classes demand more from me this term, having fun during this odyssey is still high on my list.

At the beginning of this summer session I befriended two darling blonde, elfin-type girls in their thirties. Vally, who is proficient in Icelandic—a Scandinavian language—and English, is here from Iceland to improve her French. And there is Ursula, a German from Luxembourg. Ursula works in the European Parliament and speaks five languages. She has also driven her car from Luxembourg, so we are therefore blessed with wheels, and have become a trio bent on having fun outside of school. And fun we have!

My new buddies and I have already taken trips to outlying towns. We've travelled to San Remo, Italy, and sunned topless on the beach at Monaco. Though I am slightly more endowed, I'm definitely losing the gravity battle; and my puritan upbringing did prevent me from parading my endowments in front of the other Monacan sunbathers. And with all the tanned and well-built hunks parading by on the beach, I felt it my duty to watch over my younger charges. Selfishly, I knew they could be enticed off on some adventure and leave me stranded. Age does have its rewards—and wisdom.

After being out and about in Nice for a month, it was natural for effervescent Ursula to have met some interesting people, which ended up benefitting all three of us. Her acquaintance, for example, with the sponsor of the annual Nice Jazz Festival resulted with tickets for that popular July event. We were actually backstage with the stars of the show, with Fats Domino, and rode on the bus with the musicians back to the hotel. Impromptu jammin' continued throughout the night, and my not-so-young-anymore body felt it once my head finally hit the pillow.

Our weekends continued to stay gloriously full. That is, up until Ursula decided to leave directly at the conclusion of school. That left my tan and tiny friend, Vally, who I continue to enjoy additional time with. Her vivacious spirit, spontaneity and fun attitude permeates our time together. Summer flies by, leaving Vally and I just one last get-together in Nice before going our separate ways.

My daughter, Polly, arrives July 31st. With a bag of fresh croissants in the car, she and I leave the very next day for Salzburg. After an adventurous and awesome month together, we say our goodbyes in Geneva. Polly is headed back to New York. My flight to Paris isn't far behind hers, so I'll need to rush back to the hotel to retrieve my luggage.

I enter the small foyer, and with a welcoming smile the concierge greets me. When I mention my luggage a confused look falls over his face. *Oh, God! He's lost my luggage.* It's the only plausible reason for that look.

He lifts his arms slightly away from his sides and freezes. His eyes roam to the counter and back to me, before widening into a blank stare. In slow motion his brows furrow in that universal attempt to be thinking very hard. *This can't be happening. Everything's been going so smoothly. Is this an omen?* I want to scream right here in the lobby. Forget the French!

"Think, think." I blurt out in English. I spread my arms wide to describe the size of my suitcases. "Grand, grand." I emphasize with two fingers: "*Deux, deux.*" Only a short time earlier I had asked this very same concierge to hold my luggage, while I was seeing Polly off at the airport. "*Mais certainment,*" he'd responded. He certainly remembers me now—and the luggage. So where could he have put them? It's not like I packed lightly from California. Not only did I have to send several boxes on ahead to Paris, I also have these two trunk-sized suitcases that are now missing. It isn't like you could easily misplace them.

Finally, with an 'I know where they are' gleam in his eyes, he smiles. *Thank God.*

He dashes through the front doorway and disappears around the corner of the building. In minutes, he's back, lugging my two beautiful suitcases. A tour group, evidently, was staying at the hotel and checked out soon after I had left with Polly. With so many people milling around the front desk and finalizing their bills… It isn't logical, but nonetheless, it happened that my suitcases were packed up right along with theirs and trundled off to their tour bus.

*What-if*s run wild through my head. But it's all happened so quickly that the possible tragedy of it all never quite registers. No time for that.

On to Paris!

Paris

The City of Light opens its arms to me on September 3rd. No *carnaval* greets me upon my arrival. No revelers in crazy masks. No fireworks. Sufficient is the energy inside me coursing through me, electrons whizzing through my veins. My spirit signals me that I'm still on the right track. Nice more than acquainted me with France. It provided me opportunities to make a *faux-pas* or two and to revel in the challenges of learning—all part of my training for this main event. A rush of excitement, of anticipation, envelopes me. Where am I headed? What's in store for me? It's all a mystery, but then there's still that long road of enlightenment to cover. One day at a time.

I have no trouble locating the Studio Hotel. It is just as Vally said: well-priced, clean. Even my boxes and luggage, previously sent on from Nice, were awaiting my arrival. I'm not at all surprised by how efficient and accommodating the French are. And the hotel, interestingly enough, is located just one block from St. Sulpice, in the St. Germain area on the Left Bank. After reading and hearing so much about the Left Bank I want to live here. I don't need to visit all the surrounding *arrondissements;* I already know where I don't want to live. Also in the Latin Quarter is the Sorbonne, another reason why this area appeals to me. *So far, so good.*

I waste no time heading out from the hotel down the shady side of the boulevard, flanked as usual on the streets of France by centuries old landmarks, smaller shops, bistros and brasseries. I must say, life is the same the world over. A sidewalk vender—his beret sets him apart from being an American—unceremoniously dispenses newspapers and magazines; school children sporting blue and white uniforms banter unrestrained by their bloated backpacks; thirsty Parisians occupy sidewalk chairs.

I locate a vacant seat and order a cold *Orangina* and can't help thinking how comfortable and at peace I feel arriving in this fabled city, the built-up anxiety of landing in Nice behind me. It's hard to believe that I've progressed to this second phase of my journey. It seems so long ago, when I was merely entertaining the possibility of moving to France. Now I am about to search for yet another apartment and enroll at the Sorbonne, in Paris. Another challenge. I take refuge in the fact that I can communicate now. (At this point, I could not have imagined how great a challenge it would really be.)

A momentary restlessness pulls me up and out of my chair. Everywhere I look I see somewhere I want to go inside of and investigate, something I want to stop and look at, or a cozy table to sit at to take in all the wonder. I don't want to lose a single opportunity, though I remind myself that I am in no hurry here and have an infinite number of days ahead to view as many of the antiquities as possible.

Ahead of me, the intersection curves to the left, but a slice of something out of the Middle Ages peeks out beyond a structure on my side of the street. Crossing through the intersection, I enter into a cement plaza and wonderful sounds of a huge fountain. Water cascades over two tiers, while four life-sized stone lions lie ready to pounce—mouth agape and wild eyes—and appear to be sizing me up. Above them a domed religious looking edifice with four booths, each faces a different direction and holds a larger-than-life image of a man. Four virtuous men, no doubt; the fountain is standing directly in front of a church.

Eglise Saint-Sulpice is not your typical neighborhood church. Three levels high, if I count the towers. Yet each level alone must be equivalent to three or four stories. Spanning the width of the church on the second level are six archways and a balcony. I half expect some royal to come out and 'throw cake to the peasants.' Above this pillared porch fraternal twin towers prick the sky. From where I'm standing, and with the blue sky peeking through the two outer arches, the church looks to be only ten feet deep, like a movie-set facade.

I make my way up the twelve or so steps to a massive porch, where eight pillars that Zeus could have planted stand guard about me. Each one must be 24 feet around, and instantly mine is reduced to a church mouse perspective of the world. The wooden door is as high as I'd expect, what with the size of everything else. I feel like I'm stepping through a time warp as I open the door.

Inside the church my line of vision jettisons down the nave to the front, which looks to be, incredibly, a whole city block away from me. (In reality, it actually is.) I inch my way between two sections of rows of wooden chairs. Like incense smoke my vision drifts up, up, way, way up to a vaulted ceiling of white stone. Massive leaded windows appear to recede into the stone cavities that loop out toward the center of the ceiling. Pools of natural light flood in and create an aura of holiness. I imagine angels leaping out from the window ledges and gliding from one end of the nave to the other. Four stone arches with chapels border my left and right, holding life-size statues and other artwork. I can only attempt to absorb the sum of intricacies carved into every inch of this sanctuary from the world. The silence is almost tomblike, yet I'd heard that this is home to the largest pipe organ in the world. I turn respectfully to peek over my shoulder, and there it is. No wonder I hadn't seen it, I'd walked right underneath it.

Emerging from the second floor the organ practically absorbs the entire rear wall. Rows and rows of what look like bronze pipes. Dark sculpted figures of humans line the mid-section, while winged angels and cherubs frolic at the top against all this white stone.

I turn back around and ease into one of the wooden chairs. What better place to pause and reflect.

Marilyn and her mini United Nations class walking along the Promenade des Anglais

Vally, Ursula and Marilyn

The wrapping of Pont-Neuf

The trail from Eze to Eze Sur Mer

Conversational group. Marilyn on right, Beryl center, Monique seated left

Marguerite and Marilyn

Christmas at Marilyn's. Jeanne, Vally, Marilyn, Marjie and Chris

Marilyn's Sorbunne class

Marilyn on the Champs

Marilyn and Cecile

Marilyn, her sister Loraine, and friends Monique and Karin

Marilyn speaking at Moscone Center

Marilyn at the Westin St. Francis

Jenny and Rusty at the Westin St. Francis

Fashion show at the Hyatt Regency

`LA FEMME UNIQUE`

A two hour per week, 5-week workshop incorporating all facets which make up "the Beautiful You" from exterior visual image as regards to fashion, colors, and make up to the self-visualization, image and positive attitudes as you create your own "uniqueness."

Offered by Marilyn Pearsol, former professional model and fashion consultant in So. California, and integrating into it Modern Woman's search and realization of her uniqueness.

Grow and Glow in self esteem!

Commencing: Tuesday - May 21 10 A.M. - Noon
Call: 47.20.70.86 for res. and information
Cost: 550 FF

Individual Consulting
Seminars

12

I t's already been ten days, and though I am elated to be here Paris and I have yet to tie an emotional knot. The moment I opened my eyes this morning I was pining for home. So I got up, took down a box from the shelf and climbed back into bed. I laid my head back on my pillow and started reading through letters from my family.

With each page I want more and more to reach out to them. The words blur, and I wipe away the wetness. Am I really homesick or just overwhelmed? I have been trying to absorb this big new life here. And I know I'm feeling isolated, everything's so unfamiliar. The tears continue as I read on.

They all miss me. Well, of course they do. And I miss them. Why am I reading these? I expected lonely moments. Certainly. This is more than loneliness. I have been flying rather high since I arrived, happy and confident. I think I just woke up this morning to the reality of having to find a place to live and needing to enroll at the Sorbonne. I can't put it off any longer with the semester about to

begin. Then there's the money issue and having no cushion here, no one to fall

back on. Am I fooling myself, what was I thinking? Maybe I can't do this. Maybe

I should quit before I get in over my head. Maybe I really don't have what it takes

to make it work here. What am I doing?

"Stop it! Get up and get out of here!" I order my pathetic self.

I walk over and open the window coverings. On the sidewalk below a cluster

of amber leaves lies dormant. With new life breathed into them then, they arise

and go skipping down the sidewalk, over the gutter into the street. Freedom.

I push away from the window, throw on some clothes and dash outside. I

don't even stop at the tiny breakfast area off the lobby. It's still early. Shop owners

are only now lowering their awnings and, as always, sweeping or washing down

their sidewalks. I rush down rue St. Sulpice to rue de Seine and, on impulse, turn

down Boulevard St. Michel and Pont St. Michel. I pick up my gait and hurry over

the bridge, along the Seine on Quai des Orfevres, and... I can go no further.

Met by a tranquil triangle of trees, I stand in what once was a royal garden.

Dauphine's garden. The cover of shade cools my skin, as I try to imagine the

prince playing here a very long time ago. The weight of my concerns, I notice,

must have fallen off somewhere along the way. I sit down and take in the natural

sounds, settle my gaze on the slow-moving Seine and breathe in its serenity. Its

continual flow soon calms and reassures me. I feel its pull into the present, back

into my joyous journey. Yes, joyous. I am here in Paris to continue on with what

I've begun. There is no stopping what's in motion. I just need to stay the course.

My course.

I thank my endorphins for a job well done and smile at the heavens with gratitude, as I make my way back into the early morning energy of Parisian activity. I promise myself to revisit this quiet place often. My quiet place. Well, except for the imposing presence of Henry IV astride his horse. Just the three of us then, looking out on the ever-constant Seine.

13

Approaching a second week at the hotel and having familiarized myself with the area, I felt a need to drop into the Sorbonne. I wanted to check it out and see how things were going with respect to registration and classes, only to find out that I need a visa extension to even enroll. Well, of course, since my visa will expire before the upcoming semester ends. That means a trip to the police department for my *Prolongation de la Carte des Sejours* (or visa extension).

The police informed me that I need to show them a *préinscription* (pre-enrollment) from the Sorbonne and proof of *domicile* (residency). I have neither. With enrollment dates of September 19 to October 4 coming up very soon, finding an apartment was at the top of my list, and by the 15th of this month I did find a cozy apartment in the 8th *Arrondissement* and moved my meager belongings in. (More on that later.)

Today is Monday, nine o'clock sharp. I am at the bank opening an account and transferring funds from my Nice bank. But *Mme* Bonnet, Yvette, (we are nearly on a first-name basis) does not want to transfer funds, because I do not have signed papers to establish my residency here, and my landlady is currently vacationing in Cannes. After a lengthy explanation for the urgency and the unfortunate timing, Yvette relents. *Maintenant* (thinking that my apartment is a sure thing, and all I need now is a prolongation to enroll), I hasten to the metro for another trip to the Sorbonne in the Latin Quarter, a fifteen-minute ride. This time, "*Pas possible!*" They need a copy of my high school diploma. *What?*

At precisely 3 p.m. (6 a.m. Sacramento time) I wake the household back in the states and give Dad his challenge of the day. He in turn pulls Loraine, my sis, into the act, since earlier I'd received a *coup de telephone* from her. They quickly make contact with the proper officials and, yes, the records can be sent to me. But I will have to request them by signature. *By signature...* And here I am on the other side of the world. Although now I have occasion to use DHL. For a slight—*ha!*—compensation this worldwide organization will guarantee delivery of papers to their intended destination within 24 hours. I want everyone on their toes. I call the American Consulate and Franco American Services. The following morning I put things in motion with a DHL letter to Sacramento. Additionally, since the papers cannot be delivered to a *domicile,* I make delivery arrangements to a hotel near the Sorbonne, where Polly and I had stayed.

It is utter confusion here at the Sorbonne. Everybody wants something, but nobody seems to be making much progress. Security guards line the hall in full alert and are passing out numbers with designated days for registering. There is no getting into the chamber. Since I'm armed with my copy from DHL for

95

préinscription, I cautiously (but with a certain bravado) approach a man at a lone table in the hallway. I plead my case, hold out my copy of the DHL and assure him that my records are on their way. With the help of another person who is also standing in line, the man at the table relents and obtains *number 64* for me, for Wednesday registration at 10 a.m. on the 25th of September. *Voilà!* I certainly did not tell him I am still without my *prolongation*. I'm not about to lose my precious number 64.

At 5 p.m. on a Friday the *concierge* at the hotel, where my papers were to be sent, calls to inform me that my school records have arrived from Sacramento. I celebrate with a *demi-pression* (beer) at the corner *brasserie*. The weekend passes in relative bliss.

Monday morning I walk to the Franco American Services for notarization of my school records and, "Yes, indeed, that is certainly my high school picture."

Wednesday, September 25, at 9 a.m. I am back at the Sorbonne filling out papers. The same lady sits behind the window. And "no go" this time too, because I don't have my *prolongation.*

By this time my French abandons me, and I am a blithering idiot. Thank God I'd had the foresight while standing in line to make friends with a Spanish girl who translates for me. *Enfin,* the lady behind the window slides a *préinscription* form through the little opening at the bottom of the glass partition that separates us. This form will allow me entrance to the Sorbonne, "contingent upon" (I know these words real well) my obtaining a *prolongation.* Thinking ahead at this point, I ask her for a number. On a paper with my number she scribbles *Priorite!* —and slides it my way. I smile at her, feeling quite proud of myself, then rush to the nearest metro and hightail it over to the *Préfecture de police.*

It takes a while to state my case in my terrible French, bending over the entire time to speak through yet another opening at the bottom of another glass window. I am acutely aware that everyone in the room can hear me. The receptionist slides me a number on a white ticket. I take a seat and wait. My number is eventually called and back to the glass window I go. The lady behind the glass scrutinizes my papers. If my papers are in order, I graduate to a number on a rose ticket (or blue or green) and wait some more. The object of this game, I've discovered, is to get past the white ticket, because the lady behind the window must help new arrivals; only after a spell will she even consider waiting on white ticket-holders. If I graduate to a rose, blue, or green ticket, my number will be called over a loudspeaker "*Quarante - Rouge –Trois*" (#40–red-room 3), and I'll be led back somewhere to find my *savior*, the only person in all of Paris who can rescue me from this idiocy. The secret is getting past the white ticket. Though I don't get past the white ticket this time, my papers are checked, and I learn that I need proof of *domicile* (a typed lease with copies of receipts). *Alors,* another problem.

It's typical in France for the proprietors to want to be paid in cash, to avoid taxes. Such was my case. So I called my agent, who promised to put something authentic in my mail slot. The next morning I asked Nicole, the *gardienne* of my building, if it had arrived. "*Non!*" It seems the messenger has taken it to the wrong address. Not until this evening does Nicole bring the paper over, exactly eleven days since my call to Dad.

Back at the police station this morning, it's ten minutes past nine, and I'm certain that this will be a breeze from here on out. I should be able to go immediately hereafter to the Sorbonne. I am number 58 on a white ticket and

97

feeling quite positive. I settle in and strike up an innocent enough conversation with another victim. She has to present a bank statement, she tells me. My first hint of a red flag. After two hours I numbly present my papers and, sure enough, documentation of my income is absolutely necessary. Which means I need a letter from my bank.

Back at my apartment I collect my receipts of telex monies and rush them to Yvette at the bank. "Come back at 2 p.m.," Yvette tells me. Now I am frantic about the Sorbonne deadline. At 2:30 Yvette hands me my letter, and it's back to the police station.

This time I do not sit down. I stand right next to the window, where the lady behind the glass keeps glancing up at me. She recognizes me alright and examines my papers. *Voilà!* A rose ticket. *Hallelujah!*

Two hours later, a woman—she can't be more than 20 years old—calls me into her cubicle. I am quite confident at this point, moving along in this ridiculous procedure—and my French, dredged up from somewhere, flowing as it is—when this kid actually begins interrogating me. Just when I clear one hurdle she presents me with another. She is "cyu-rious," why am I going to school in Paris, at my age? (I'm trying to be charming, really.) Finally, she agrees to give me a *prolongation* to October 31 "on the condition" that I check back with her, with whether or not I get into the Sorbonne. *Oh, my gawd!* Then she asks me to write on a piece of paper my parents' names, where I was born, etc. She looks at my name. She looks at the name of my parents. "Why are they different?" she asks. Hmm, how can I prove I am their daughter? I shove my hand into my briefcase and yank out all my school papers that date back to grade one. I pile them on her table. I point to my parents' names. I point to the dates. And, oh, yes! I point to my high school picture with my name printed under it—all verified by the Franco American Services. That does it. She understands. All I need now are black and white photos. Next stop, a photo cubicle in the next building.

I pop in *5ff*, wait five minutes, and *enfin!* —the reluctant piece of antiquated machinery coughs up my photos. I now have my *prolongation de Carte des séjours* and enroll at the Sorbonne, exactly two weeks from the day I called Dad. I was told subsequently that it might have been easier to enroll at the Sorbonne if I had not been living in France. Also, in retrospect, I was very naïve in writing to the Sorbonne from Nice for an application, and then in due course, sending a check drawn on the Banque National de Paris.

14

During the chaotic enrollment at the Sorbonne, I was answering ads for furnished apartments. Most are bleak with decrepit upholstered furniture and velvet drapes—reminiscent of some unfortunate soul down on his luck during the Napoleonic era. Newer apartments are just too tiny. The other apartments seem to cower in neighborhoods I wouldn't think of living in. And for my peace of mind, liking where I live is critical. I just need to keep on looking. So many *arrondissements* to choose from, and I am not the only American who's searching.

I spend one afternoon with an agent and a businessman named Brad, who is also looking for a more spacious, more *haute* apartment. At the end of the day neither of us finds what we want. We part ways but not before exchanging phone numbers and promising to be on the lookout for what each of us is looking for.

In the newspaper is an ad in "Le Figuro" that looks interesting. Though the apartment is unfurnished (I was not considering buying furniture) I think I'll see it anyway. My agent, an American expatriate who has spent ten years in Paris, has connections. *This looks promising.*

Situated on rue de Bassano, which intersects and is one and a half blocks from the Champs-Élysées, the apartment is a short walk from the Arc de Triomphe. The *Huitième* (eighth) *Arrondissement* is a clean and vibrant area. The apartment sits inside a large corner building comprised of spacious apartments. Better yet is the 5-digit security code. Also, a *gardienne* inhabits a small apartment just inside the entrance, which is great. And though the facade is rather unimpressive, it has a stunning foyer with long, narrow marbled floors and sections of mirrored walls that give the impression of a ballroom. A further stroll along the hallway, with two steps leading up at lengthy intervals, leads to another of those birdcage elevators. As it climbs, an elegant wrought-iron staircase comes into view, miraculously attached to a curved wall.

On the *troisième* and top floor I step out to view my possible future residence. This master suite is closed off from the rest of the apartment with its own entrance (ingeniously installed) in the outside hallway. Upon entering the living room (originally, the master bedroom) I find nooks and shelving with built-in drawers. Continuing on under an arched 13-foot ceiling is what had once been the dressing area, now the kitchen space with a built-in unit on either side of the bathroom door. On one side stands a stainless-steel sink and cupboards. On the other side squats a sufficient little range and a midget fridge huddling beneath it. If anything, I find this place strangely appealing. But there's more.

The living room window has a view, albeit to a quiet car-lined street below. But a view is a view. Nice light comes into the room softened by colorfully striped awnings over an intimate wrought-iron balcony. But the bathroom, larger than the living room, is the *piece de resistance.*

High ceiling, well-lit shower stall, separately-lit tub, a bidet and a regular ol' fashioned toilet. Flashy, too. Quite the showcase tiled wall-to-wall in *wake up!* Canary yellow. Clean and airy. The whole apartment shouts 'Paris!'

Now that I have an apartment and I'm ready for school to begin, I need to address some basic furniture and other accoutrements, to at least make my stay in Paris enjoyable and comfortable. Luckily, the previous tenant offered for a reasonable amount a cream-colored double sofa bed. The only piece of furniture in the entire apartment. Sleep and study, possibly the only things I'll be doing here. And as it was in Nice, no cooking or dining in this apartment until I shop for kitchen things. Groceries and a couple inexpensive pots and utensils should suffice, since I don't consider perfecting my cuisine. As for furniture, something funky and fun but unique. A little *haute,* yet inexpensive.

For the most part, I've succeeded with my decor. I settled on white wicker chairs with fanned backs to accompany a circular wooden slab with screw-in legs that comfortably seats four. I covered the table with an off-white, floor-length cloth. And to set the mood for my Parisian scene, I placed a black-shaded, black ceramic lamp on my off-white table cloth. *Perfection.* But dishes, and glasses to drink my French wine, are another matter.

Growing up I had the chore of drying the dinner dishes. Always anxious to get back outside to my awaiting friends I'd rush, and…well, thank goodness for *melmac* that just bounced off the linoleum floor and showed not the slightest bit of offense. Good thing our 'company set' was relegated to the china closet and off limits to my hand-drying tendencies. Over the years I have progressed some; and since there are no linoleum floors here, maybe I could risk a little more *haute* than *melmac.* With that decided I am ready to shop. Boy, am I ready.

Not to shop while in Paris is, well, out of the question. Not even to be considered. After all, I rationalize, I only shopped for essentials in Nice. With that smidgen of guilt silenced, three locations come instantly to mind: Galleries Lafayette, Printemps (both department stores) and the Place Vendome featuring individual stores. So, I'm off to the Place Vendome (a 17th Century French architectural square housing academies, the National Library, and residences for ambassadors and other world dignitaries). Nearby on rue Royale unique stores await the discerning buyer.

After strolling along rue Royale for some time, I realize I've been craning my neck for a look-see in the windows and wondering—Is this only a lesson in futility?—when displayed in a storefront *vitrine* I see something unusual. I can't believe my eyes. Six gorgeous plates, each rendering a different slender woman modeling turn-of-the-century fashion. Each plate is also numbered. In moments, I leave the store with six dinner plates and six salad plates of Villeroy & Boch, circa 1900 and wonder, will my cooking do them justice?

Further browsing produces some delicate glassware sporting clouded stems. Inexpensive bedding, an armful of colorful pillows, assorted art posters, and a futon complete my living room. Now I'm set for my cozy Paris hideaway.

Back at the apartment the futon goes directly into the dressing room, which will be my bed when guests stay overnight. For my gem the yellow bath I bought black terry cloth material, which I set about immediately hand-hemming for towels. Black and yellow. How could one be in Paris and not be a little flamboyant? Now I have a home.

15

While October brought the beginning of school, it also heralded a change in the weather. The sun softens earlier. Sometimes it completely disappears under low-hanging overcast skies that grow more and more somber, until darkness envelops the city. An eerie mist slithers up then, from the river to the street lamps, and casts reddish haloes over the boulevards. It's another world after dark. But I enjoy how the tempo beats so differently from that of the daytime. And living so close to the Champs Élysées I feel safe enough. My favorite destination? The grand and luminous *le Drugstore* in the shadow of the Arc de Triomphe, located roughly four blocks from my apartment. Packed with all sorts of goodies, from the medicinal to the frivolous, it is more than the name implies. I shop alongside other night strollers just as reluctant to bid Paris *bonne nuit*. Weekly mornings, on the other hand, run on the predictable rhythm of ritual.

Each near-dawn the alarm clock gets me up and about my morning ministrations: a thank-you meditation, a shower, maybe some yogurt and a banana, then off into the pre-dawn darkness for a short walk along the Champs Élysées. After two blocks, I venture down into the truly dark bowels of Paris for the metro, in which several passengers and I sit trance-like until our underground destination. From there we disembark and scurry through dimly lit tunnels past vendors hawking their wares and, eventually, resurface into the still-dark Parisian mist— like rodents venturing out from our holes. My destination? Boulevard St. Michel.

I follow along the bank of the Seine.

The Seine... It reeks of centuries of use, lost lives, and eons of waste. The muddy, unforgiving flow advances along its course, an innocent receptor of untold atrocities. What forbidden secrets it must hold. The river begs forgiveness for its part in receiving spoils of hundreds of decades of abuse. Yet its mindless, soothing surge forgives all and accepts its destiny—a landmark of truth.

From across this flowing dark mass the bells of Notre Dame toll out the hour. One... Two... Three... Eight reverberating bongs. I stop to gaze at its illuminated Gothic towers and listen. I feel heaven's angels all around me in what feels like timeless, unnatural peace. This spiritual something stays with me for two blocks more. It lingers as I step inside the building of education and clump three flights to my classroom. It lingers, until I fix the ear-phones to my head and hear the first drone of "*Maintenant étudiants. Répétez.*" The exchange of realities is instant, and repetition is my world for the next several hours.

Now because my fellow students and I are here to learn French and do not have the privilege of actually being schooled on the hallowed premises of the university, we attend off-campus sites referred to as satellite classes. These classes are scattered around the Left Bank and within walking distance to the Sorbonne. This is our training ground: the earphones, the endless repetitions of French phonetics, and the playback of those passages again and again. We have volumes of work to wade through before we can even think of diving into the depths of the revered bastion of history and knowledge, which is the Sorbonne. Once Phonetic class is finished for the day, my classmates and I stroll singly or in groups for several blocks down Boulevard Saint Michel. Sometimes we stop *enroute* for a croissant before entering another building, through another set of imposing wooden doors, to climb yet another stairway to our next classroom. More aptly, a petite auditorium. And since I want to focus without someone sitting in front of me, I feel it necessary to stake out a seat in front.

My desk, front row and center, has a writing surface in front and slightly to my right, where I meticulously straighten my recently purchased notebooks. I pluck a pen from my purse and glance at the low stage in front of me, where my diminutive instructor stands.

Unlike Marie Cécile, *Mme* Brouchard wears a Sonia Rykiel design, just as I wear boots and a long skirt, not jeans. I also observe that she has noticed the obvious age gap between me and the other students. We have fourteen countries represented here, with only one other student from the United States. Scandinavia, Asia, Australia, and with one student, even Yemen is included. (This is how I collected coins from around the world and would later give them to my grand-daughter, Ashley.)

While lacking the intimacy of my class in Nice, these students, nonetheless, are friendly. And while each of us significantly expresses ourselves in French (a breakthrough for me), some of us occasionally meet after class for *café* at the

Place de la Sorbonne, a plaza adjacent to the university. Considering our diverse backgrounds and the little time that has passed so far, I'm pleased we are quickly becoming friends.

The class work, while not a breeze, surprisingly, does not overwhelm me. *Mme* Brouchard assigns homework each day, and each Friday she tests us. I receive my fair share of corrected papers and still remain a comfortable and eager student. In no time, the French is flowing from my mouth and seems second-nature. Instead of nervously straining to translate, some mechanism in my brain has finally clicked. If one word doesn't register, I still understand the gist of a sentence. To say the least, my confidence is soaring and so is my interest in my scholarly surroundings.

Since I am a student now, it behooves me to do a bit of research. I learned that the Sorbonne was built in 1253 to simply accommodate 26 theology students. The university consisted of a loosely knit soapbox/street-corner-lecture-type education, with students living haphazardly in inns throughout Paris. That all changed by the end of the 13th century, when the Sorbonne became the administration headquarters for the University of Paris and housed 15,000 attending undergraduates. It comes as a surprise to learn that the university (during the 100 Years' War, from 1337-1453) actually sided with England and recognized Henry V as King. Later, in 1642, when Cardinal Richelieu became grand master of the Sorbonne, he instigated the restoration of its dilapidated buildings and replaced them with a Jesuit-style church, the first Roman-style building. During the revolution the university closed and did not reopen until 1806, when Napoleon made it his Académie de Paris. Over a century later, in 1968, the students revolted, and the Sorbonne was rechristened 'Paris University IV.' Presently, the only part of the 1642-built Sorbonne remaining is the chapel, where Cardinal Richelieu is

entombed. His remains lie inside the sealed tomb today. I can visualize the tomb

and a stone replica of Richelieu half-reclining on his white sarcophagus, his very

real-but-threadbare cardinal's hat dangling from the ceiling. Tradition has it that

once the rotting threads snap, his hat will plunge to the floor and release

Richelieu's tormented soul from purgatory.

I've procrastinated long enough, but now I knew it was time to face my own

torment—an obscene amount of cash I owe to the Internal Revenue Service.

I called Franco American Services for the proper procedure for paying U. S.

taxes if one is out of the country. I should have known. 'Go to the American

Consulate.'

After a quick call for an appointment I arrive with all my papers. But getting

into the consulate is no easy mission. They have security checks everywhere. As

one glass door closes behind me another check point awaits me. Having an

appointment merely 'got me in.' I present my papers and am asked for my ID,

including my visa. From here, a single guard accompanies me into an elevator

(just the two of us) to another floor, to the small office of the man with whom I

have my appointment. After looking at my papers—twice—this man hands me a

slip of paper and directs me to another area. Time to pay the piper. With great pain

(the only way I can describe it) I write out a personal check for the entire amount.

Not a cashier's check. Not a certified check. My personal check. I am surprised

this doesn't concern them, but I guess they know where to find me. With my

account rapidly depleting, it is incumbent upon me to be seriously frugal. Herein is

the challenge, not to spend money while in Paris.

16

I t seems my arrival in France has had me connecting effortlessly with just the right person who leads me into yet another experience.

My call to the American Consulate resulted in a young, personable woman who referred me to the Franco American Services and an American affairs spokesman who, in turn, directed me to the Women's Institute for Continuing Education (W. I. C.E.). W. I. C.E. is connected with the American University of Paris and originated (for women like me) to assist new arrivals in Paris through various social activities, lectures and courses. Comprised of a dedicated staff of volunteers (mostly wives of businessmen assigned to Paris long term), these women help us newcomers to assimilate into the Parisian scene by guiding us and making us feel welcome and comfortable. She further advised me of an invitational tea the following Sunday, for new transplants. What luck! As this happens only once a year.

The morning of the tea and my introduction into W. I. C. E. elaborate pains are given to my toilette, as if I'm about to be presented at court.

Inside the tea room my first encounter is with Rita, the wife of the executive editor of the *International Herald Tribune*. While a loose bun remands her salt-and-peppered hair, she overflows with serenity and friendliness. In fact, she oozes with charm and class. She would become my introduction into the finer life of Paris, an incomparable sojourn.

The tea was superb. And afterwards, Rita called and asked if I'd be interested in joining her and some friends for an afternoon Japanese flower arrangement demonstration, in Neuilly, an affluent suburb of Paris. Earlier in my life, I had neither the time nor the inclination to pursue this art form. (And as it turned out, I got to meet several French women and an American lady, Beryl, the wife of the U.S. Deputy Chief of Mission—assistant ambassador to France).

Following our afternoon in Neuilly, Rita called with yet another invitation. There exists in this world-class city a group of women (twelve in all) who meet weekly for tea and conversation. Since one English-speaking participant has recently left, an opening is available, and my afternoons just happen to be free. Of course, I jump at the chance to be a part of this fascinating assemblage, a distinguished milieu.

Six of these women are French, and six of us are English-speaking though not necessarily American. We do not meet merely for refreshment and camaraderie; our conversations commence for the first hour in the language of the hostess and, after which, we continue in the other language for another hour. There is no program, just women getting together to discuss the week's events and trivia. And I mean trivia. The sole purpose here is to learn how to better interact socially in a language not our own. Some are more eloquent in their mastery of the other language, some of us are not. And as we converse it is perfectly acceptable (in fact, expected) for one of us to correct the others' language skills. I decided to give a dissertation in French about an afternoon bus ride I'd had. I was a little out of my comfort zone and noticed them smiling, though no one said a word to interrupt. That is, not until my friend, Monique, said, "Marilyn, did you really take a ride on a fish hook?"

A beautiful and talented Parisian, Monique is the spitting image of our famous dancer and movie star, Ann Miller, and also loves to dance. Becoming most friendly and helpful since we've met, she and I are becoming close outside of the weekly tea group. Other distinguished French ladies are professional women or the wives of French executives of American corporate affiliates. The six English-speaking ladies are just as diverse.

Young Maureen from Ireland (married to a Frenchman who subsequently found, and left Maureen for, a mistress); some wives of American corporate executives, usually assigned to Paris for three-year stints; a woman from Beverly Hills, California; and me. (It was through Helene though, the wife of a French corporate executive and a member of this club, who would thrust me into the orbit of one of the most famous Parisian *haute couture* designers of all time.)

Although this group met on one occasion in my tiny apartment, we mostly held our gatherings in the larger homes. It presented a rare privilege to view the intimate living quarters of such diverse and interesting women.

Monique's flat opens up into a living room with 13-foot ceilings and three sitting areas, incorporating plush purple sofas with aqua velvet curved-back chairs. Her living room bears an Asian influence, with its irreplaceable artifacts and a collection of jade that befits a museum. At one end of the living room elaborately-painted oriental screen doors stand as high as the ceiling and unfold to display a magnificent extended mahogany dining table set for tea. I've since visited her place often and treasure these Parisian moments.

On some occasions, our group travels by van to some interesting site of historical significance in or around Paris. While one of the French ladies acts as docent, the other ladies assist. What a hands-on experience these outings are. This special circle of women of whom I have grown to respect nurtures a refined and reserved friendship, always respectful, always well-dressed. But it does lack the intimacy and informality we might experience in our American counterpart.

Also available to me through W. I. C. E. is a monthly bulletin, where I can avail myself of courses, events, outings, and innumerable other items of interest. I even enrolled for a 12-week art course in Impressionist Artists. Not that I'm interested in an art career, but I am here to discover things about myself. Middle-age should not be a barrier to enlightenment. (As I found out that there was a Monet and a Manet: both impressionists.)

So far, this art course is proving to be most enlightening. I feel tremendously appreciative of the art that so prevalently absorbs Paris, which reminds me of something I saw during my first week in Paris.

Walking from my hotel one morning towards Pont Neuf, I noticed that half the bridge was being covered with what looked like bright yellow fabric. Not loosely draped but tightly bound, like a bandage on a wounded limb. I was inquisitive, sure, but didn't grant too much to it. This is, after all, Paris. Not until I read in the paper the following morning that the famous artist, Christo, was 'wrapping' Paris's famous bridge did I take more interest.

Pont Neuf, the "Heart of Paris" during the 1600s, was the first bridge in Paris not lined with 2 and 3-story houses. Its designer wished that all Parisians be able to view the water. Over several days I'd been watching Christo bringing his masterpiece to life, as if it were some piece of furniture to be reupholstered. Finally, and on an especially sunny morning, Pont Neuf was utterly transformed. Hundreds of uniformed pleats spilled down from the top of the bridge and tucked tightly under the long walkway, then streamlined down the legs of each arch. Like gold-leaf in sunlight, the bridge blazed against an ultra-marine sky, its gilded reflection shimmering over the ever-brooding Seine. *Spectacular!*

I guess that was my first lesson in Art Appreciation.

Also, Paris, being the hub of earth-shattering events in and around Europe, has no shortage of internationally-known speakers. Richard Bernstein of the *New York Times*, having just arrived from the Reagan/Gorbechev Conference in Geneva, spoke to us one evening. But not every female transplant living in Paris seeks such creative and stimulating outlets. Americans here with businesses, families or romantic involvements are otherwise happily occupied and stimulated by their endeavors. They are not seeking outside interests. But I'm single, older, and don't yet have a social base, so my involvement with W. I. C. E. is tremendously broadening. And I can't help comparing my life here to my adventure in Nice, how these experiences are becoming bolder in scope, more challenging, more meaningful and soul satisfying.

17

O ut of my original association with W.I.C.E. there emerged other individuals into whose orbits I've been providentially cast. One of the services within W.I.C.E. is a counseling class. Rather a gathering for support. Women presently relocated to Paris and needing emotional assistance in coping are invited to come join in the meetings and be guided through their situation. Moving to Paris under any circumstance is a huge undertaking. And once the uniqueness wears off (as with one wife who really didn't want to leave her family and friends for so long a stretch of time), a period of adjustment follows on its heels and help is needed. An American woman with a Ph.D. in psychology, and is married to a French banker, chairs this counseling class and has asked me to assist. I don't envision myself as a wizened old soul yet, but being that I am older, maybe she thinks I've attained some great maturation. In any case, I gladly jump in.

During these classes I meet Karin, a previous United States resident who's been involved in a long-term relationship that went sour—how providential that the City of Light beckons wounded souls and heals them with its light. Obviously, our connection was instant.

Karin is an intellectual type, of medium height and slight of build and with long blond hair that frames her glasses. What draws me to her is her curiosity, her friendliness, and her interest in life. Both of us troubled spirits were drawn to Paris and a desire to find our paths. Therein may be the piece that links us. Anyway, her hunger to learn has been challenging me.

Then there's Marjie who I finally meet. I say 'finally,' because for several weeks now Karin has been saying, "You have to meet my friend, Marjie. She's thinking about going to Nice, and I told her you used to live there." It's not that I've been avoiding Marjie, my plate just happens to be full. But one evening the phone rings and it's Marjie. She wants to know, can we meet for coffee? Regardless of it being a school night for me; and regardless of the fact that I'm right in the middle of studying, I agree to meet. It would be rude to put her off any longer.

Now everybody who visits Paris knows Fouquet's, the famous gathering place at the corner of the Champs Élysées and George Cinq. Known in its glory days as a rendezvous for Paris' literati and those in the art world, these days Fouquet's is merely a magnet for tourists. Still, for a pricey cup of coffee you get to gawk at the international guests as they go sauntering by. But near Fouquet's is a smaller, more intimate Café Select—a short, safe walk from my apartment. We agree to meet there.

At a bare rattan-type table in a small, glass-enclosed room surrounded by green potted plants, I see an attractive young woman enter in and look around. Must be her. A natural beauty (about five-feet, seven-inches tall) with reddish hair, this refugee from the corporate world, and recently of San Francisco, radiates warmth and serenity. What was only supposed to be a short visit—giving her hints about life, and living, in Nice—ends up being a three-hour gabfest. I've never believed in accidental meetings, and this rendezvous is no exception. Our paths were meant to cross. And lately, during my down times, Marjie and I have been spending a lot of time together. It's plain to see that I am becoming as much of a lifeline to her as she is inspiring and giving me a much needed solace. Like young school girls, we dash through the Marché aux Puces on some carefree excursion, laughing like we were the only two people around. We thrust aside the leisurely strollers and experience lighthearted, loving moments and wonderful adventures together. Thus, Karin and Marjie have become another spoke in my friendship wheel, the first being the conversational group, of course.

Reflecting on the close relationships being forged, I ponder over being bereft of close friendship in my early life. I wonder too what is making the difference now. Was I just too busy with Johnny, the kids, my job? I'm just as busy now with school and adapting to a foreign country. I don't know. I only know that I am in a most awakened stage of my entire life. What an unforeseen blessing of middle age!

A third spoke begins with Constance, another American, who has been living in Paris for ten years. She belongs to a small group of women who've been meeting each Sunday at different restaurants for lunch, and she's invited me to join her.

In addition to discovering new eating haunts, this encounter leads to an introduction to blond and cheery-faced Chris, who is more my age and also hails from Southern California. Chris is an accomplished artist who has excelled in impressionist painting in oil. She's in Paris visiting her daughter, Jeanne Manson, a singer and actress who is married to a French actor. Since Paris is the perfect setting for Chris's artistic talent, she has since obtained her own apartment, and this allows us to spend more time together. The bonds of friendships here and in Nice, I'm discovering, are strong and sincere. Blessed to have these friends is the fortunate part. Speaking English regularly now is unfortunately working against my dedication to learning French. Lately, I'm only speaking French at school with my classmates. To counter this, I enroll in a separate French-conversational class of about eight students, offered by the university and taught by a teacher at the Sorbonne. He speaks no English whatsoever.

18

Many women fantasize about having an affair or a romantic interlude in some exotic city, such as Paris, Rome or London. I could not fathom that such a thing would be on my horizon. But I am headed for just such an experience. It happens quite accidentally.

The phone awakens me. The fluorescent 9 on the dial of my clock tells me that I've overslept. I clear my throat.

"Hello?"

"Marilyn, hello. This is Pat, how are you?" The agent who negotiated my rental—so out of character for her, making a friendly call like this. "Are you available for dinner this coming Friday evening? I'd love to take you to this darling Russian restaurant, where you can savor something other than French cuisine."

Mais certainment! —as I am wide awake now, and my calendar has certainly been lacking in social engagements. I assure her with a groggy yes that it would be fine, and she can pick me up at 8 o'clock.

Located off of a quaint cobblestone *allée,* we find the restaurant tucked away in a cellar. Already I'm loving this. A short flight of steps lead down into an electrically-charged atmosphere. I don't know Pat that well, but I sense I am in for a good time. A colorfully-dressed waiter guides the way to our table, where a gentleman just happens to already be sitting. Waiting, it appears. Instantly, I recognize him. It's Brad! He stands and greet us with a resultant look of recognition, though he appears just as surprised to see me here. Even more amusing is Pat, who is noticeably interested as to how we apparently know each other.

"Well, I see that I don't have to introduce you two." Brad and I look at each other, smile, not knowing who will speak first.

"Actually, this is our second meeting," Brad offers only a crumb. "We spent one afternoon being driven around Paris." Pat's mouth hangs slightly open, her head bobs waiting for more. Brad doesn't take the bait, so she looks at me and raises her eyebrows. Curiosity is killing her, I can tell.

"We were thrown together while looking for an apartment," I explain, and Brad looks directly at me.

"And apparently you didn't find one suitable for me."

Okay, he's a kidder. Apparently, since Brad and I had both used Pat's services, we are two satisfied customers being rewarded with dinner.

Colorful vibrancy swirls around us, while rich, nuanced tones permeate our conversation; I've been swept up and set down in a cellar somewhere in Russia.

And am I really here with a man I barely know? As a vice-president of a large American corporation, Brad Evans has been assigned to their Paris office, in charge of international sales in several countries. I assume he's only just arrived, as he was also looking for accommodations when we'd first met. I notice the beads of perspiration across his forehead and upper lip, but the food isn't spicy. *Heat from the fireplace? Something more?* My mind is charging.

"I made a miraculous find," he volunteers. "It's a classic two-bedroom apartment in a rather stately building, right on the Seine." I look at him. (Or, am I sizing him up?) I tell him how marvelous this is, and of course, there is the jousting of banter that follows. Pat speaks up.

"I visited friends in Paris ten years ago, fell in love with it, and here I am helping you two move here." In those years Pat never married, but she's built up a following, mostly with referrals from the states. How propitious that our hostess angel is rewarding us this evening. I ponder the odds of both Brad and I finding this obscure agent in a Paris newspaper. At evening's end we leave happily satisfied. It was like having a blind date with a chaperone.

One week later I get a phone call. It's Brad, *naturelment*, and, would I be interested in exploring the Marché aux Puces—Paris's famous flea market? I'd been there before with Marjie, but I hear myself saying a little too gleefully, maybe desperately, "Oh, that sounds delightful." A little while later I open my door, and a schoolgirl crush comes over me. I am giddy at the thought of spending the day with him.

The metro is a way of life for Parisians. Once mastered, one can travel in minutes from one end of the city to another. With the vast miles of tunnels below, it's amazing that Paris doesn't collapse into its bowels below the streets. During inspections (I read about this.) tunnels did sometimes collapse. They refer to those tunnels as the 'buried past.'

We disembark at the Cliqnancourt exit and keep a look-out for the gypsies, whose haven this is. Continuing on for several blocks in a tunnel under the *périphérique* (the circular highway that surrounds Paris), the first stalls come into view.

Making our way through the dust and din, hordes of humanity announce their presence with the customary bartering in full swing. Boisterous foreign chattering fills the air, coins and currency passing between hands.

"Did you know that this flea market had its genesis in the late 19th Century?" he says. "By 1920, actually. Today there are more than 2000 stalls." As we pass the stalls I see furniture, bronzes, secondhand goods, clothing and antiques—ever mindful of the gypsies milling around. Still, I am having such a wonderful morning. We lose track of time browsing and inhaling the dust stirred up by treasure seekers.

"I can see you're dying from exhaustion. What say we have something to eat?" He didn't have to repeat it. I look around but see nothing suggesting food. He takes my elbow and, leaning down, whispers in my ear. "Come with me, *Mademoiselle*." I float along attached to his arm, afraid I'll drift away if I let go.

We come upon an unimpressive barn-like structure with a barn-sized wooden door. Brad opens the big thing to a cacophony of voices and blaring music. Up on a balcony stands a petite, black-haired singer dressed in blue sequins and warbling Edith Piaf. All thoughts of the flea market have vanished, as I'm pulled decades back in time to a war-torn Paris. This is Chez Louisette, a haven for locals who savor an atmosphere not unlike a speakeasy. Aside from the French songbird on the balcony, long tables with benches are jammed together and cover the entire floor.

Brad cups my elbow as we nab a seat, join quickly in the camaraderie, and even shout out our order. The waitresses obviously cannot get to all the patrons— and this is really the fun part. Someone shouts above the din an order of chicken and beer, and the waitress returns and slides the pitcher, the mugs, and the orders down the length of the table. When our order stopped before reaching us, a friendly patron looked down the table our way. I'm yelling, "*Ici! Ici!*" (Here! Here!), and the very nice gentleman gives it a good shove and sends it further on to our outstretched hands.

All sound is momentarily muffled. I venture deep inside myself and consider how it is that I am with this beautiful man in this untouched-by-time place. I glance around as if from the outside. Patrons eating and laughing and clapping to the wonderful music. I steal a peek at Brad. Here it is again: I'm setting foot on the tarmac in Nice; I'm sitting next to the restless Seine, alongside the statue of Henry IV astride his horse; I'm hearing the bells of Notre Dame tolling out the hour; River mist is swirling up and painting my first Paris night.

Filtering back in with full volume the timbre of voices, the resounding laughter and glass mug bottoms thudding on the table tops—immersed in this moment, I am more alive than I've felt in a long time. I finger a savory piece of chicken—grease on my hands and face—and wash it down with a dark and wonderfully bitter beer.

Our song bird is still trilling as we get up to finally leave. We close the big door behind us and make our way back to the market. There's something about this place that keeps us browsing. Maybe it's not the market. Maybe it's just me not wanting this time with Brad to end. Either way, I spot a bright orange, featherweight silk scarf for the bargain price of 10ff ($1). It's mine. *And what are these?* Pictures of seductive, red-lipped beauties dressed in black. How perfectly they will adorn the walls of my apartment.

Eventually tired of the jostling and the noise but with energy left to expend, I hear him say, "Let's get out of here." We retrace our steps to the metro and disembark at the St. Michel exit, in the heart of the Latin Quarter. With no destination in mind, we wander along the banks of the Seine and along a line of battered stalls that look quite out of place amid the rest of the architecture. Reminiscent of hotdog stands the way they lift up in front.

"These are the *bouquinistas*," Brad tells me, "independent book sellers of prints and rare books." 'Rare' gets us burrowing our way in through elbows and hips to unearth our own treasure. In earlier years a significantly valuable piece of history would surely have been available for the diligent miner. But for all our digging we come up empty. The near-impossible odds have certainly not stifled their market, thanks to those original dealers centuries ago who bucked the traditional book sellers and made a market for themselves right here in these battered green stalls.

In a neighborhood *tabac* at a small table we cap our friendly date over wine. Sitting side-by-side, Brad's hand brushes my hand and his eyes dive into mine. I am warm through and through. I look away.

The day could not have been lovelier, and I have a strong feeling that there are more to come. I feel a little dizzy with happiness. *Thank you, God.*

19

"Some weekend," says Brad. My breath catches at the sight of him.

"Pardon me?" He's caught me recalling our first meeting and, how deliberately he carries his tall, medium frame; how irresistibly European his trench coat and slightly rumpled, curly black hair; how he strides into the reception area to where I am sitting; what confidence and success he radiates. *Is he really not married?* I glance once more—nope, no wedding ring. I'm in love. What does he expect now, since our flea market date? Did he expect such electricity between us?

Near the Grand Palais and hidden well behind an overgrowth of foliage, a romantic dinner awaits us. *How did he ever find this place?*

Inside the Theatre du Rond-Point, from the center of our table-for-two, candlelight flickers. Nearby subdued conversations barely permeate my consciousness. This is the place for lovers. And his manners, the way he seats me and inquires of my comfort. I cannot take my eyes off of him with his tan leather jacket and black turtleneck underneath. Black curls play around his collar.

"Would you like to visit the castles around Paris some weekend?" Wow. I'd heard about the beautiful castles.

"Why, yes, I'd like that very much. I've looked forward to visiting them. Sounds great."

We continue our invulnerable repartee, discussing the local neighborhood street markets—when he does have time to shop. And yes, he is especially fond of the French cheeses. But no, he does not speak French and doesn't plan to learn. I realize how challenging and demanding his job is, the more he talks about it. It must be near impossible for him to maintain a steady relationship with all his traveling. He covers Germany, France, Belgium, and England.

He asks what brings me here to Paris. I ask him the same question. I give only the cliff notes' version of my unusual adventure, and he…well, he just works a lot. The dinner is excellent and we drink lots of wine, and so I am finding it difficult to speak intelligently. But it doesn't prevent me from pondering the possibility of yet another adventure with him. I do not want this to end.

Far from ending, it isn't long before the wellspring of desire erupts, and caution swirls away like the mists from the Seine. It does not seem strange that neither of us ever offer nor question the really private parts of our pasts. It seems irrelevant that I am divorced with two grown children. I assume he must have been married at one time too, he's so attractive and has so much going for him. So far, we've just been living in the moment, never really anticipating getting serious. At least, I'm not.

This is working out perfectly, and it leaves me the time to pursue my many interests and then, look forward to seeing Brad on his return from his many business trips. Sometimes he'll call around 10 p.m., after having just arrived in town, and ask if I've eaten dinner yet. We dine in modest-but-romantic restaurants —always off the beaten path. Secluded, would be more apt. It's a bit of a rush to discover these hidden places. Sometimes we go for a beer and *croque monsieur* (the French grilled cheese sandwich). Even these *tabacs* are far-removed from mainstream Paris strollers. No one, I mean no one, has a clue of my affair with Brad. No one would chance a run-in with us anywhere. (My silence will prove to have been a wise choice.)

After a Sunday morning cup of coffee at his place, Brad and I decide to take a leisurely stroll along the Boulevard d'Alma, adjacent to the Seine. It's autumn now. The air is so crisp it nips. It also works up an appetite. Unbelievably, there isn't a hint of traffic this morning. Still early as we head for the restaurant at Pont d'Alma for breakfast—arms entwined around each other's waists—wind-whipped leaves rush between our legs and whirl around us. I think that Brad takes this as some kind of cue, when he playfully pulls me toward the center of the boulevard.

"This is crazy," I tell him. But his face is beaming.

"I've always wanted to do something radical like this," he says. Before I realize what's happening he takes my hands and pulls me into him. In the presence of God and the quiet world around us, right in the center of Boulevard d'Alma, he plants a time-stopping kiss on my lips. A feeble mutter escapes me, when the only motorist on the road honks at us. However, at this moment, this may just be worth getting hit by a car. Definitely a kiss to carry me through my weekly rituals at school, with W.I.C.E. and the other outings I take, until the next time he's back in town.

Yes, my life here is steadily evolving into a satisfying and comfortable pattern. My angels are still on my shoulders. In some ways, it seems I'm living some fantasy existence. But it is real, only barely outside my dreams. I leave my apartment each morning, greet the *gardienne* and take my usual turn toward the Champs. The two Russian guards that flank the nightclub reluctantly send a smile my way; how can they not smile to me, this high-flying female who is bubbled in nothing but positive energy. Nothing can ruin my days. Not for the time being, that is.

20

After having a television in Nice I did not want one here. Having already been so well-immersed into the language, I didn't think it would further my proficiency in French. Instead, at home in the evenings, I insert my miracle cassette into my Sharp player. (I call it a miracle, because wherever I am in the world it picks up any local radio station.) I dim the light, lie down on the soft carpet and turn to my favorite drama station. Here in the murky glow of my abode I am instantly absorbed into the evening's play. Much like *The Green Hornet* of my early childhood radio memories or *The Shadow Knows*, where doors *creak* open and shut, footsteps *tap* across barren floors, whispered lovemaking and violent arguments. These current dramas unfold through my earphones, and I am thoroughly engrossed. In this atmosphere there is no struggle to translate French, I am living it.

After weeks of my no-English/French-only classes, I'm beginning to think in French. Even in my dreams at night I'm speaking French. During the day, I notice that even my responses are becoming more French; it's not just a conversational thing. I find myself mimicking French inflections and animations. As '*oui*' means 'yes,' I've noticed Americans peppering their conversations with 'yes, yes' or 'right, right.' No sooner do I enter into a conversation in French, the inevitable '*oui, oui*' pops out. Just agreeing with a natural enthusiasm. But when I'm not studying or attending other functions, here I am at home reading or enjoying my theatre.

I really do feel like I'm a limb of the body here. Attached. And why shouldn't I? I'm connected into so many facets of Parisian life: I'm going to school; I'm socializing, even dating; I attend concerts and church. Just one of them now. And living so close to the Champs Élysées and the Arc de Triomphe seems to pull me into their everyday experiences or the dramas that are more unique. Such as a parade, of which there are many, and they happen right here on the Champs.

One day, an obscenely huge flag appeared out of nowhere it seemed and was covering the entire center of the arc. When I'd inquired about it, a local filled me in with how some head of such and such country was visiting and, "We are honoring him by hanging his flag from this prestigious place of ours." Normally, for a patriotic event the flag of France would be draping over the Arc. Representing each of the twelve battles won by Napoleon are twelve avenues that each lead up to the Arc. In 1923, soldiers lit the flame to mark The Tomb of the Unknown Soldier. The Arc de Triomphe is more than a landmark, it is patriotism living on in every French heart. (Some months later, in July, I was headed for the Champs and found crowds lined up and down the boulevard. People were yelling and pumping their fists into the air. All I could see over the heads in the crowd were helmets speeding down the boulevard. I didn't want to miss a thing, so I elbowed my way into the pulsing throng. "Q'*est-ce que c'est?*" I asked a bystander. "*C'est le Tour de France!*" he told me. I couldn't believe it. I just happened to be standing at the final stage of the famous bike race—I would actually return in 2000 to see the entire finish of the Tour de France with my granddaughter, Ashley.)

21

Always curious and not usually in a hurry, sometimes I can take an unscheduled bus trip across town and back, and feel totally carefree and satisfied. While other things I do inadvertently plunge me into a bout of homesickness.

From the bus one day, I decide to follow a handful of passengers, just to see where they are going. I follow to the top of a hill, where a nice grassy mound ringed with stately trees exposes a peaceful view. From here the grass slopes down the other side to a nice lake.

I take a seat on the cool grass and breathe in the serenity. A flock of ducks play tag, while two pearl-white swans glide uninterested across the lake's surface, swan-sized Vs trail behind them. But down by the edge of the lake and close enough to see his own reflection, squats a little boy in navy-blue pants. In his little hands, a miniature sailboat. Still squatting, he gives a little shove and watches the sailboat wobble some inches from his hands over the calm water. He steals a quick glance back at who I assume is his father, who is reclining on the grassy bank. Their smiles mingle and register profound love. Suddenly, I want a hug. I want to share a smile with my family, so very far away. I feel the urge to rush back to my apartment and scribble out an emotional letter to them, let them know I'm thinking of them and missing them. With this deep need for a hug, I allow my thoughts to regress to the circumstances that had originally set this particular odyssey in motion, the fear and depression that had temporarily crippled me. I am not that person anymore, and I refuse to be homesick. That is not why I came to Paris. I shake it off, stand up, and make my way back toward another foray into discovery.

With a little help from my Michelin guide and Parisian friends, I brave into the strange and mystical places, allow Paris to capture and absorb me and not let me go. As its captive, I am led through the haunts and mysteries secreted in the *allées* and streets of the *arrondissements*. Thoughts of home set aside for now.

22

Attending the Cordon Bleu was never my mission in moving to Paris. But an appreciation for French cuisine is fully ingrained in me by now. I dine out often with friends. We discover quaint eating places then pass the word. The *nos Ancetres les Gaulois* (our ancestors, the Gauls), located in the heart of *Ile St. Louis*, is at the top of our list for group dinners. Raucous and fun, as its name implies, they serve fresh farm food on trestle tables, in candlelit rooms under huge-beamed, vaulted ceilings. Large baskets of *crudités* (raw vegetables), baskets of bread, hard-boiled eggs, pickles, and other delectables. We help ourselves from a huge wooden cask to all the wine we can drink before our food arrives, while a guitarist sits by a rustic fireplace and strums nothing but flamenco music. We usually float out of here just in time for the 11 o'clock metro.

A Paris restaurant's *pris fixe* dinners are really the most economical, and I am supposed to be frugal these days. A three-course meal means an appetizer, *entrée*, salad, cheese, dessert and wine—all for under 100 *ff* (or $10.00). Rarely do I order *biftek* as the meat is tough. Not at all like our tender sirloins and filet mignon's in the United States. But I do enjoy rabbit, fish, chicken, and *only the way the French do it* dishes. I've fallen in love with the *crêpes* sold at the corner *crêperie*, filled with Nutella and Grand Marnier. To counter all the waist-disfiguring *pâtisseries* available, my friends and I visit the abundant *fromageries* with some 350 different cheeses. We just taste our way to heaven, *trench* by *trench* (piece by piece). Occasionally, at lunch I pop in at a *brasserie* and order *crudités*, which come with bread. And there is no bread like the French baguette eaten without butter, crumbs falling where they may. I can easily devour half of one, while sipping the perfect red wine of the day.

Accompanying my eating experience, it's not unusual for a French-loving dog to be squatting nearby and studying each morsel that vanishes into my mouth; his little tongue wets his lips, primed to gobble up whatever might fall his way. Eating establishments are quite dog-friendly. In fact, dogs are more welcome than children. This then, is my eating experience here.

Honestly, my focus is not on food, though I have been taking notes on how to turn out a proper French meal with the help of a friend and without attending the Cordon Bleu. Chefs can spend what would feel to me like days in the kitchen, to prepare some exotic dish. Chefs also have *sous* chefs and a few kitchen helpers. The everyday-busy woman has no time for that. So here's the secret: substitute. A lot of our American products will produce the same results, especially in sauces. I've been able to turn out some truly nice dishes, once I'd found the right substitute. The following is a classic Americanized French appetizer that Monique served at a luncheon.

Oeufs en Gelee (Eggs in Aspic)

Cover six eggs with cool water. Bring to boiling and boil four minutes. Remove from heat and set under running cold water. Let stand until eggs are cold. Peel and place one egg in each mold (custard cup or muffin tin).

Dissolve one envelope of gelatin in heated beef bouillon (10 ½ ounce can). When cool, pour over eggs. Refrigerate until firm.

Unmold each onto a bed of watercress or lettuce. Serve with mayonnaise.

As a new bride at nineteen my culinary expertise consisted of canned Franco-American Spaghettios or Pork'n Beans with frankfurters. Over time, I graduated to meat loaf and tacos. But after preparing my first turkey dinner, no one was more surprised than my mother-in-law when Johnny was carving the beautifully browned bird and discovered the plastic bag with the neck and giblets still tucked nicely into the cavity.

While my weight loss began in Nice, it wasn't because of a conscious decision to go on a diet. My lifestyle here has been so different from what it was back in the United States. My focus now is not on food or dining, in spite of the countless references made about dining out. In Nice, almost everything I needed or wanted was within walking distance. I only rode the bus to visit Marguerite or take trips to outlying sites of interest and the university. The ideal location of my apartment made *mostly walking* possible. That hasn't changed in Paris.

It's been my ritual and a terrific convenience to stop at a neighborhood street market on the way home from school, pull out my collapsible tote bag, and fill it with fresh produce, eggs, cheese, and fish. I go to the regular market only to buy staples. And from the moment I first laid eyes on the phenomenal French pastries peering up at me from behind their glass-enclosed cases (begging), I vowed there and then not to over-indulge. Every few days, if I feel I've punished myself enough, I let down my guard after dinner, push aside my conscience and savor some luscious Napoleon or cream puff. Who wouldn't?

There are two desserts I'm particularly fond of here: *Profiterolles* and *Îles des Flottant*. I do not remember tasting these dishes before moving to France. *Profiterolles* are medium-sized cream puffs (*Pâte a Choux*) stuffed with ice cream or buttery whipped cream and drizzled with dark chocolate sauce. Cream puffs are made from scratch here.

Îles des Flottant (Floating Islands)

Simply, egg whites (sweetened) beaten stiff and dropped by mounds into a hot, vanilla flavored and liquid-like custard (a little thicker than eggnog). Cook until egg whites remain firm. Serve mounds of egg white with vanilla sauce in a soup bowl.

This dessert is awfully rich but I like decadent desserts. And it wasn't only with food that adjustments have been made since coming here. There is also the subject of drinking. It basically has to do with culture differences.

Back in the states, while I was single and in the workday world, I did, unashamedly, frequent the popular 'happy hour' festivities held at various restaurants. Bombay or Tanqueray Gin on the rocks with free appetizers was the tonic to dull the wits after a week's work. Usually I had two. This has changed in

France. To my knowledge, this custom is nonexistent, as I don't know anyone here who drinks hard liquor on a regular basis. The scene is different. Wine is the drink of the day, with the house wine inexpensive and delicious. Cocktails are certainly available at restaurants, usually drinks consisting of *apéritifs*, wines, and *liqueurs*. The *apéritifs* have also varied over time. Some typically French light drinks I've come to enjoy: *Vittel-menthe* (*Crème de Menthe* diluted with *Vittel* water) or *pastis* (clear anise-based drink). I've settled in for 'the wine way' of France. And so far, France is very good for my body and my spirits

23

The days are shorter now. November has blown in bringing with it some dreary overcast skies. But today the sun has broken through. And though it's too late to see the full spectrum of fall colors, I'm still taking the metro to visit the Bois de Bologne. I was instructed from back home to be sure and experience the changing of the leaves.

After exiting the metro in Port Maillot and walking only a short ways, I know immediately that I've entered the wrong end of the Bois, far from the miles of bike and walking trails I should be seeing. An area of three square miles on the border of Neuilly makes up the Bois. "You'll know once you enter into it," I was told, "the forest is dense" —a myriad of trees altered over the years, to make way for lakes and grassy meadows and miles of trails, a race track and, more recently, restaurants and cafés. I wind my scarf around my neck, pull it up over my mouth to ward off the chill, and walk into the brisk day.

In the distance the first sparse copse of trees comes into view, most of their branches already bare. A vast area of naked trees stand stark against a backdrop of sunburst yellow and bronze. Indigenous trees in late bloom elbow evergreen pines. I continue wandering through the Bois over gold and red-but-bruised, dampened and dirty leaves. The end of the season is not the time to visit. I guess I expected this. I plod on, wondering if there will be time for me to return here in the spring, when a curled leaf cuts the air in front of me and settles where I'm about to step. Then a wind gust sends falling all around me a host of these lifeless reminders of previous days.

I make my foray deeper into the woods feeling more flushed with each step. Through the foliage in the distance someone stands. No, two lovers with arms entwined as one. Though I am willing to share this day and this beauty, I am content to be alone. I feel at one with this universe here, shaken loose of dormant cells and feeling such freedom from the chaos that was mine. Awakened wide-eyed to the magnificence around me I find this another day to just *be*. Who would've thought a simple walk in the woods could do this? Disappointed not to have seen the Bois in its full glory, yes. Rewarded, nonetheless, I make my way back to the metro.

The first snow of the season falls.

I open my shutters to a white world and can barely catch my breath. I have never lived in snow as an adult. I rush through breakfast, apply my soft contact lenses (as is the norm), dress warmly and head on outside.

How strikingly quiet it is.

How untouched and beautiful against such a dark and brooding sky.

A current of frigid air whistles past my ears, sending fresh powder skirting across the snow.

I start out at a leisurely gait, never anticipating any trouble, only the sound of wonderful snow crunching beneath my boots and compressing under each delightful step.

The Champs-Élysées looks so alien with everything shrouded in white. The familiar Russian nightclub…no burly guards flank its doors; closed, and much too silent. Only muted snowflakes falling now with some regularity.

At the corner I stop and glance both ways. Not a soul. And since I live closer to the Arc de Triomphe and go that way often, it is towards the Place de la Concorde and the Tuileries, in the opposite direction, that I head for.

Along the otherworldly Champs-Élysées—absent of color and definition, lines of full trees all shrouded in white—I continue past avenue Roosevelt. I recall events that transpired along this great avenue: the honoring of heads of state, parades, the bicyclists of the Tour de France; marching, striking students, Napoleon with his army, German tanks… I can almost feel their presence.

An impressive blast wraps the hem of my coat around my legs. Undaunted, I press on down long blocks toward the square, Place de la Concord, with the Jardin des Tuileries (public gardens) just beyond.

The 'Place de la Concord' wasn't always called that. After the Revolution the square was renamed Place de Revolution. During that time the guillotine was the weapon to eliminate the unfortunate. 1119 people were executed from 1792 to 1795. Louis XVI and Marie Antoinette were beheaded right here, in this very square. But wealthy neighbors on rue Saint-Honore complained that stale blood, still seeping from the stone, was ruining their health and devaluing their property, and so the executions were discontinued. I shudder at the images and keep walking.

The expanse of the Tuileries looks like a deserted graveyard, with a lone bent soul trudging towards me. A lingering gust *slap, slap*, slaps the hem of my coat against my legs. The man strains to hold his hat to his head, while a veil of snow hurls between us. It's difficult to walk straight. What was I thinking, coming out in this? The snow is really coming down. I can barely make anything out in the distance.

The wind howls again, and I don't need another warning; I turn to head back for home, but the wind drives the snow into my face now, and I can't even see my footprints. I try to pick up my gait, but it's like walking in knee-deep water. I strain to see ahead through the slits of my gloved fingers. My contacts...they're so cold it hurts to blink. Little tornadoes of snow make it difficult to navigate. A hidden curb... I slip and nearly fall. *Focus straight ahead! Watch your footing!* The pain... My eyes are getting worse. My contacts are going to freeze to my eyeballs. *Will a doctor be available?*

My heart is racing by the time I'm home inside my bathroom and soaking a washcloth in warm water. I lay it over my closed eyes for several minutes before attempting to remove the lenses.

That was scary.

My face has not been so fortunate. Why didn't I think to put on protective coating?

I immediately apply Vaseline, and soon enough—yes, I am back outside—I continue with my explorations and hope to keep out of trouble. And still applying my Vaseline.

24

The holiday season is upon us. The streets are strung from one pole to another with colorfully-lit decorations. Across the Champs and in all the shop windows Christmas beckons. My favorite time of year. And since this is to be my first Christmas away from home, I look forward to making plans with my new friends.

Red-cheeked pedestrians rush past, as Beryl and I head home on the metro, following a festive tea at Rita's home. We couldn't have been in a happier, more carefree mood, when the car approaches its next stop and the doors open.

A man who'd been standing next to me suddenly bolts past me, and I feel a slight tug on my shoulder. In the time it takes to look down and see my purse unzipped with no wallet inside and look up again, he is long gone. How irresponsible of me! Here I'd left my purse openly unguarded, hugging my load of gifts and paraphernalia with one arm and clutching the dangling metro strap with my free arm. This can't be happening. And right before Christmas.

My whole body is shaking. I try to stay calm but my thoughts replay what just happened. I look over at Beryl, as if in a stupor.

"I've just been robbed."

"What—how?" In seconds, my life is turned more upside down than I'd first realized.

In my wallet was my driver's license, credit cards, *carte d'étudiante*, metro pass, and about twenty dollars in *francs*. Most importantly, my visa.

Once at home, Beryl calls me with the number to notify for lost credit cards. I call immediately, and they will issue new ones to me. Thank God, for Beryl. More than once she's answered questions and come to my rescue. (During a bombing and subsequent anti-American sentiment, she advised our American group to keep a low profile, not to display any signs of the United States, while businesses were being told not to fly American Flags. She is the gal in the know.)

Since I am already enrolled in school, I don't really need my *carte d'étudiante*. I notify the school anyway. My driver's license I can replace when I go home on vacation. But the visa… That is another matter. I know it will be impossible to obtain a duplicate, having previously gone through the nightmare at the *préfecture de police*. Nonetheless, I go there to see if I might find the same person who'd waited on me the first time around. It should be much easier this time.

No such luck. I go to the same window, but a different person sits here. And as soon as I'm handed the proverbial white slip, I know I'm in for another rough ride.

Sure enough. After starting the whole procedure, it will now take a month and a half before they notify me with an appointment (one and a half weeks hence). Oh, and I should bring my divorce papers with me at that time. *Divorce papers?* They weren't necessary before. Then the perfect solution comes to me. I'll go to the police station (the local *gendarmes*). Not to obtain a duplicate visa, but to report my stolen wallet. Sure, the police can't be bothered with a mugging or robbery, 'it happens all the time.' But that's okay, I only want to establish my stolen visa and obtain from them a report attesting to all this.

My French comes in handy while cajoling and explaining my problem, my schooling and travels. Finally, they give me such a report with the understanding that I am to obtain a new visa. At least I have the report. With this accomplished I feel safe. I carry the notice with me from the police, in lieu of a visa. Incredibly, this solves that problem. It turns out I don't even have to obtain a new visa.

With the robbery behind me I'm savoring every minute leading up to Christmas. I didn't buy a tree, but I did manage to find a strong-smelling pine bough, and I'm using plenty of candles to create a holiday atmosphere. Brad will be spending the holidays in the states, but since I'm not the only one spending the season in a foreign country, I've been making wonderful plans. I received calls from Vally in Iceland and Ursula in Luxembourg. Vally will be coming to spend Christmas with me. Then the three of us will meet in Milan and travel to Venice for the New Year. I can barely wait.

As our plans evolve, so are the plans of my friends in Paris. Marjie will be in town, as will be Chris. Things are shaping up to assure that no one will get homesick.

Two days before Christmas Vally arrives. High with happiness and enthusiasm, we waste no time popping the cork on some good French wine. We soon settle down to catch up and make plans during her visit. We go window shopping along the Champs. We savor roasted chestnuts in little paper cones offered up by a smiling street vendor. Everyone is in the Christmas spirit. Such a magical time. We agree, it is a must that we go to midnight services at Notre Dame Cathedral. It doesn't matter that neither of us is Catholic, we want to experience the sacredness of Christmas. But first that evening we plan to attend a party at a friend's apartment. And most rare of all invitations is an invite to my *professeur's* home. I just knew that our close proximity in class would eventually benefit me, and I was not mistaken.

On rare occasions, when students were not deluging her with questions after class, *Mme* Brouchard would open a conversation with some casual comment with me, for I'd felt it presumptuous of me to initiate. This gave me the opportunity to have a one-on-one conversation with her. I commented on her stunning outfit. That's how I knew she wore Sonia Rykiel. Then, on the last day of school before vacation, she had asked what I was doing over the holidays. I mentioned that a friend was coming down from Iceland and that we would be meeting another friend from Luxembourg in Milan, to spend the New Year in Venice. She was intrigued and asked if I had a place to stay? "No, not yet," I'd told her. She suggested I drop by her home at 7:30 the following evening, and that she'd be happy to give me the name of the quaint pension where she liked to stay. To say I was pleased would be inadequate. Profoundly flattered is how I feel, that she allowed me such intimacy. Never could I have imagined being invited to a

Sorbonne *professeur's* home. But that is exactly where Vally and I find ourselves at 7:30 that evening.

Mme Bourchard and her husband, a dentist, greet us cordially. I expect a brief encounter in her foyer, to receive the desired information and be escorted back out the door. But no. She offers us an *apéritif.* While she has previously ascertained that I am a grandmother, she now seems intrigued about my meeting Vally at the University of Nice, and further, that we are on our way to Venice. Taken by her hospitality and friendliness (albeit stately), it is a challenge speaking social-conversational French with this lady of position and prominence, but one that quickly evaporates with her graciousness. I'm also suddenly aware that the generation sandwiched between the students in my class and me—Yvette, at the bank; the French ladies in my conversational group, store clerks, my university professors—does not speak English. Most are highly educated, so I can only gather that English was never mandatory in their schooling.

In due time, two children with impeccable manners are ushered forth. With their tiny outstretched hands they make our acquaintance. How early formalities are taught. Before coming to France I'd heard such negative comments of the French, but my experiences are proving them all wrong.

By the time Vally and I reach the Cathedral tonight, the magnitude of the crowd overwhelms me emotionally. That so many would brave the cold and sit out here in it…

There was never any doubt that we would be listening to the service from outside, so we search the Place de Parvis for a spot and squeeze in. Shoulder to shoulder with the jostling crowd, we listen as somber organ music resonates from multiple outdoor speakers. With the Seine so close by and the late hour, a wet mist hangs in the air. Little puffs of fog issue from the mouths of the faithful gathered round me. Fortunately, we've dressed for it. Interspersed with the fog and the litany of Latin opens a dimension I slip into but rarely experience. The deep notes of the organ hum inside me, and I no longer feel the cold. Just a strong, spiritual connection with this congregation and with God. A serenity that doesn't come often enough. Eventually, though, the crowd disperses, and with their going is severed our tangible connection.

To markedly lighten the mood however, Vally readily suggests we take a look-see at a little jazz joint across the river on the Left Bank. It must be 1 a.m. by now but we go.

What were we thinking sitting here with glasses of wine, listening to music at this hour? Time to go home! But how? While we'd taken the bus to the cathedral, it was unthinkable that we hadn't thought about transportation back other than hailing a cab. But our little walk across the Seine fixed that. Too late! With today being Christmas Day already—and I am expecting a full house—I didn't want to be out all night. But it looks more and more likely that this will be our destiny.

We rush back under fog-obscured street lamps, across the Petit Pont, to begin our unplanned jaunt toward rue de Bassano down empty, ghostly streets. The click-clacking of our heels on the wet pavement echoes in the eerie silence. An occasional bus and even a scarce-but-crammed taxi swish by, but they don't stop. It seems the entire city of Paris has evacuated, except for us and the handful of lucky ones with transportation. Or maybe they're all cozy under their covers and dreaming about presents under their trees.

So here we are, two weary and foolish women making the long trek back home. No longer concerned about the time, we can only think of perching on the side of my tub, soaking our feet, and maybe indulging in a little Grand Marnier.

Christmas day is up and running. So am I. Jeanne Manson, a strikingly beautiful American girl with flaming red hair that frames her porcelain face, has a surprise for us. She's presented each of my guests with a ticket to the matinee performance of her play "Le Sexe Faible," at the Théâtre Des Arts Hebertot. Jeanne is also an actress and the daughter of my artist friend, Chris. Just as Broadway does in New York, little theatres abound in Paris. And since dinner is scheduled for late afternoon, this is the perfect suggestion.

And planning my festive table, there couldn't be a better time than now to use my Design 1900 china. In lieu of a turkey (impossible to find), I'm serving smoked salmon wrapped around hearts of palm on a bed of greens, with caper vinaigrette dressing. The main course will consist of tiny game hens with herbed wild rice and a voluptuous cheese platter. My long stemmed glasses will bubble with champagne, while tiny plates of scrumptious desserts from my neighborhood *patisserie* will complete our holiday feast.

So it comes to pass that I spend my first incredible Christmas abroad with such an interesting group—my eclectic spokes of friendship: Chris, Jeanne, Vally, and Marjie, sharing dinner, a play, and warm camaraderie.

25

O n to Venice.

It's still the holiday week, and Vally and I are meeting Ursula in Milan, where we all embark for Venice. The land of the 'Lagoon Dwellers,' the former Veneti, who joined Italian forces to thwart the Lombards. I have always wondered why a city would literally be built over water. Now I know. The Venetians had no choice.

To withstand the attacks and save themselves from the barbarians in the 7th Century, the small fishing villages along the Adriatic coastline combined forces and took refuge amongst the Islands of the Lagoon. In the 8th Century, two merchants smuggled the body of St. Mark out of Alexandria, Egypt, and brought him to the home of the Veneti, known then as Rialto. St. Mark became the Patron Saint of the city, and the Veneti became free men.

Our train pulls into the Santa Lucia Station, which happens to sit on a spit of land that juts out into the sea. We disembark and push our way through the frazzled Christmas remnants of celebratory souls, past vendors and hawkers, and on through the exit doors to a waiting *Vaporetto*—a slow moving water bus that stops umpteen times along its route. Rather than descend into the congested interior, we settle on the open deck, maneuver our obstinate luggage and brave the cold, moving air. I glance at my Venice book and locate my *professeur's* instructions: *Pensione alla Salute (Da Cici)—station La Salute.* Apparently, this is our stop.

Along the water route we pass gondolas nestled in their foggy blankets, sleeping side-by-side in their cribs. We pass the Byzantine facade of a palace, enchanted by its beauty. There are Gothic, Renaissance, and Baroque architectural masterpieces along the way too, each one a reminder of Venice's past. We see the arched bridges, under which the gondolas and all of Venice's service boats pass.

All too soon then we arrive at our stop, trudge to our awaiting Venetian hideaway and settle in. We are here for such a short time it will be impossible to visit all the places *Mme* Brouchard has suggested: *la Ca' d'Oro, le Musée de l'Académie* and *le Musée Corer.* But her note does say: *Il faut boire quelque chose au Florian ou au Quadri Place San Marco.* (Be sure and have a drink at the Florian in St Mark's Square.)

Unfortunately, the weather is proving to be at odds with what this romantic city should be like. But what did we expect coming here in the dead of winter? Luckily, Venice isn't experiencing high tide; at least we can mingle with the pigeons in St. Mark's Square without having to wear rubber boots. I wonder if that *doge* of an earlier century ever regretted releasing those gifts from the balcony of the Basilica over the Square. How these birds have proliferated over the centuries. I ponder whether their protection now causes much chagrin to the Venetians and the tourists.

From our small terrace at the *pensione*, and because the weather took a nice turn overnight, Vally, Ursula, and I take advantage of some rationed sunlight this afternoon. Revving their motors and breaking the languid silence are the frequent service boats puttering by. Since there are no cars, these service boats are the life blood of Venice. In spite of them, what a tonic for our souls to set our faces to the sun in this respite from the fog. Even if it's for such a short time.

With the eve of the New Year upon us and no plans or reservations for dinner, we decide to walk until we find an inviting restaurant in which to celebrate.

Bundled in woolen coats and Ursula in her fur, we venture down numerous deserted passageways. From the canal, the mist rises like souls released from a watery grave. The fog presses down low and drapes us in its mystic world, as we cross over one arched bridge after another to who knows where. We pull our scarves tighter around our necks and keep walking, our noses glowing scarlet now with cold. Just as we comment on our meandering jaunt being no more than a lesson in futility and feeling more than a little impatient, we spot a welcoming eatery. The windows are fogged, the place must be packed.

We open the door and see that the patrons look to be enjoying themselves. This definitely appears to be the place.

Inside the reception area the warmth envelopes us, and tantalizing smells tease our senses. It is 10 p.m. and we're starved, but no tables are available. Undaunted, we ask our hostess for a bottle of champagne and, 'may we enjoy it right here in the reception area, since we are its sole occupants?'

So here we are, having a great time—our one bottle almost drained—when our hostess reappears. She bends down and, glancing back through a glass partition to a table of diners, informs us that an Italian family has invited us to join them. My mouth drops open. How wonderfully munificent! They undoubtedly feel sorry for us. (A testament to the friendly Italians.)

She leads the way to where we join our hosts, who are by now finishing up their dessert and coffee. Once they depart for the night we do not let the food-speckled tablecloth deter our enjoyment of a champagne dinner. We order a fabulous Italian meal fit for the hungry celebrants that we are. Midnight arrives and with it a new year, starting off with lots of singing, shouting, clinking of glasses, and kissing amongst the amorous Italians. The revelry continues. *Viva, Italy!*

With the holidays over, another event is scheduled, which I'm not looking forward to.

26

I awake with a start.

I look at the clock. I've overslept! —this of all days, my Sorbonne exam.

Scheduled at the end of each semester, the only place and the only time for this rigorous exam is held on the outskirts of Paris. I won't be able to make this test up. How could I have overslept? Has all my schooling been for naught because of something so stupid?

Fighting off panic, I dash around not knowing what to do first.

"Be calm! Be calm!" I shout to myself. It's bad enough that I've always been a lousy test-taker. Fear of not passing always resulted in lower test scores. *What if I fail? No! Stop this right now!* I will break that cycle today. *Just focus.*

Three days ago, some classmates and I had taken a dry run on the metro to get all the stops and transfers down. It took three transfers, but I hadn't made a note of it, because we were all to meet this morning and travel together.

I grab my test instructions, purse and backpack, rush through the door, and run to our meeting spot. *Oh, my gawd!* They've left without me.

Surrounded by strangers, I will myself to recall the names of the transfers. I have faith that I will remember. The worst that can happen would be missing the test. Worse-case scenario? I don't pass the test. But I am not going to quit and be defeated. Just focus on one stop at a time.

I hop on the metro and force myself to scrutinize the map in the curve of the car's ceiling. *I know that name.* Sure enough, it is the first transfer. I let out a sigh of relief and slightly relax.

After disembarking, I head through a tunnel to gain the other side of the tracks. Shortly, another train arrives going in another direction. I board this train, and another name seems to pop out from the map. Another sigh of relief, confident now that I will know the third transfer as well. And I do.

After disembarking once more and gaining the street, I run-walk two blocks to an imposing building with very impressive stone steps. This is it. I slow down. I pull in some deep breaths.

From outside in the hall the testing room looks more like a bare gymnasium, except for the long tables set a few feet apart. We're instructed at the door to leave large purses and backpacks before entering.

From the positioning of personal water bottles, apples and other snacks, some seats are already taken. I take a middle seat in the second row. Each place has a pencil and instruction sheet. My heart thuds against my ribcage. All my childhood test-taking rushes back at me.

We take our seats. In the eerie silence I glance around. No one else appears to be breathing, let alone speaking. An occasional scrape of a chair breaks the anticipatory hush. I hear the footsteps of our instructor coming forward, and she stands in front of us. She gives some verbal instructions, and should we not understand she invites us to ask our questions now. Far be it from me to break that silence for clarification. (In French, to boot!) I surrender to anyone brave enough to do so. At this point we begin.

Several monitors commence roaming the aisles, glancing side to side. Thank God I took a middle seat. Just what I don't need, a monitor brushing past me every few minutes. Each segment of testing is timed, and how naturally the old rules come back to me, which I rarely followed anyway: scan the test, respond to the questions I know, repeat the process until I've labored over the questions that need more attention.

A slight shuffling of papers disturbs my focus, and I see a monitor escorting someone out of the room. I swear, the tension in this place is unbearable. But this is no time to speculate. Only the grind to quietly look inward for answers and complete the test. One glance at some of these questions sends a shock wave through me. *How can I possibly answer that?* All segments of my schooling are being tested.

At last, it is over. Whether I passed or not, the experience alone of having attended the Sorbonne will be unforgettable. I also chalk up a positive mark for not having succumbed to fear and panic. Thankfully, it's over.

Getting up to leave, I see two empty seats that I remember previously being occupied. Were they unable or unwilling to continue? Once more, I'm glad I followed through to the end. Now for the results, which will be posted on the main bulletin board, in the corridor outside of the office.

The very next day during finals week I am scheduled to take my oral test. While having coffee with some students in the Place de la Sorbonne, another classmate stops by to inform me that the test scores have been posted and that I've passed. On the outside I'm sure I look calm. But profound relief, joy, and, yes, a great excitement shoots through me—like in a pin-ball machine, it bounces off the walls inside me. During a special ceremony one week hence, I will receive a diploma, or rather, Certificate of Completion.

It's finally here. I feel like royalty with each step up this wide and impressive, curved stairway to an upper floor of the Sorbonne, to an auditorium used only for special occasions.

Through double wooden doors we enter the auditorium. To the left of the stage is a curved area with graduated, elevated seating. Inside this centuries-old domain of learning we continue creeping up bowed, wooden steps to our seats.

The cavernous room is only partially filled, as we wait for the ceremonies to commence. From this perch on the second tier, I watch the administrator on the stage giving the necessary greeting and formal congratulations. My heart kicks into second gear. He reads off our names one by one, as each student rises, walks down the aisle to the stage, receives his rolled up diploma, shakes hands with the administrator, and returns to his seat. Finally, I hear it.

"Mar-ee-lyn Peersol." Shaking all over, I lift myself from my seat and make my way over the knees that jut into the path to the aisle. I manage the remaining steps to the stage and find myself face to face and shaking hands with the administrator—my diploma held tight in my other hand.

Cours de Civilisation Française de la Sorbonne

Certificat de la Langue Française

Niveau élémentaire

Yes, this was the elementary level, but the ultimate prize for all my efforts.

As I hold this simple document in my hand, resurrecting those early thoughts of insignificance and insecurity I know my feelings of inadequacy are gone. I absorb this moment of new-found accomplishment and humbly realize that I'm just one microcosm in the vast universe. The thought spirits me back in time. A friend and I are lying out on my front lawn under a canopy of flickering stars. I follow his finger, as he traces Orion's belt and the Milky Way. He points out the North Star. My teenaged problems—naturally blown out of proportion—shrink under such vastness. In one sense I feel minuscule beneath this twinkling expanse, yet I desperately want to rise to some kind of greatness. I'm in awe; the view inspires me. And at this minute, in this respected institution, I make my way back to my seat, knowing that centuries of real scholars have walked these sacred halls, climbed these same steps and crossed this wooden floor to receive their own diplomas. It is no big thing for an academic to receive yet another rolled-up scroll, attesting to his widely-known brilliance. But for me, from my humble beginnings...

I started working at fourteen in the basement of a department store, typing envelopes during school breaks. Engaged at seventeen and married two years later, I epitomized the 'poster wife' during the decade that followed World War II. I worked full-time then, putting Johnny through five years of college. Yes, this diploma is special. Never having any previous university experience and receiving a diploma in a foreign country—and in that country's language—is huge. This is awesome.

27

The *tap, tap, tap* on my door late at night announces Brad's arrival. After four months, my feelings for Brad have intensified, just as I know his feelings for me are becoming stronger. Instead of calling me from Paris at the end of a business meeting, he's been calling me from Brussels or some other city the day before his departure to alert me. I leave my cozy blanketed burrow and pad to the door, clad only in my nightie, eager to see his tousled curls and playful grin. Our eyes lock in mutual desire for a lingering embrace.

"If you think I'm fixin' you somethin' to eat this late, it ain't gonna happen," I say.

"*That's* not what I want. But a cold drink would be nice." It's a short distance to the fridge for an *Orangina.*

"You okay?"

"I am now. It's just been a rough few days. I couldn't sleep on the flight back from Frankfurt. You?"

"*Je voudrais que...*" I climb back into my bed and watch him.

"Ah, come on, Smarty, you know I don't understand French. Though I kinda like what I think you were going to say."

"You think?" The bantering stops. He lifts his right hand and places it gently on my left shoulder. His pinkie slides under the flimsy strap of my nightgown and wanders downward. I feel the strap gliding down my arm, his warm, big hand following suit. I lean back into my pillow and watch as he sheds his last clothing. I trace my fingers across his back. I ask no more questions. His skin is soft, not an athlete's body. His demeanor is gentle, and with him I feel safe. But if it is I who is to be his haven in the stormy sea of his life, so be it. Brad's eyes bore into mine, there is no mistaking his desire. He reaches over and turns off the lamp. Insulated from the rest of the world in our secret, warm womb, I smell his faint odor of manly sweat. Time does not exist as we hungrily seek out our longing bodies. Finally, we sleep locked together, until the darkness of early morning, to awake and go our separate ways.

28

Because of my stolen visa in December, I imagine that continuing classes at the Sorbonne will not be possible. However, I want to stay on in France, and that presents another challenge. I'll need to think of something to do to justify living here. Of course, thoughts of real estate come readily to mind, but those days are past. Something new lies ahead. I just need to discover what that is going to be like. And the way I keep meeting the right person all along the way on this journey… Who is it who will provide the missing piece that leads to my tomorrow?

Days turn into weeks, and the weeks are ticking off the calendar. But I haven't missed the steady decline in the dollar-to-*Franc* relation. Very soon, I'm afraid, I'll be facing a dilemma for which I am not prepared and do not want. I'm not ready to go home. Leaving now would suck all the resolve that I've put forth to discover that for which I've come. But I cannot continue indefinitely nipping away at my financial cache like this. I need to reevaluate, and soon. I will work something out. It's just not time to leave Paris.

Surprise, surprise! Marjie's just accepted a position at the Château de Lesvault, in Onlay, in the center of the Burgundy area. She'll be visiting the château next weekend, and I am going with her. Seems my life continues in a perpetual state of unexpected adventures. I keep looking out for the moment of truth, the one step that leads me into my new calling. I'm close. I feel it. I just need to keep putting one foot in front of the other and follow, as opportunities continue coming my way.

Early Saturday morning Marjie and I catch the train for Nevers at *Gare de Lyon*. I'm looking forward to a fun weekend.

In Nevers, we grab a snack before boarding the bus. After an hour or so of serene countryside, we are let off on a deserted country-road intersection and told to wait.

Not a single street sign, stop sign or street light. I'm not too concerned, as we strictly asked our driver about our destination; he assuredly nodded his head that this is the place. Right in the middle of nowhere. Albeit a beautiful, undulating, green-pastured nowhere.

Marjie re-reads her directions, as this is her first time to the château other than by car. Just when my apprehension is about to get the best of me, by gawd, a bus comes ambling up the long road, and we climb in.

After another scenic haul past typical farmhouses with low rock-piled walls and four hours behind us now, the bus pulls into the little village of Moulins-Engilbert. The owner of the château, driving a vintage American station wagon, stands waiting by the vehicle to transport us.

The Château de Levault turns out to be a classic French manor of the early 19th century. It's as if time passed over it, nestled as it is in the middle of a wooded park. An intimate lake sprawls along the backside. Peacefully set in gorgeous countryside halfway between Paris and Lyon.

Ironically, an American couple had purchased the place and restored its eleven tastefully-furnished guest rooms. Inside the social room, comfy old chairs and couches fan out in front of a fireplace—already stacked and burning with wonderful heat. Seems we were expected.

We are welcomed with a *kir* (white wine and *crème de cassis*). My first taste of the traditional French drink. Because the château boasts its own chef, its popularity obviously demands some attention to the kitchen, where Marjie is destined to be their *sous-chef* for the foreseeable future. My good fortune as her good friend destines me to visit her. So it is arranged that I will share her room and pay only for my meals.

Ages before France had come into the picture, I had developed a passion for *escargots*. Whenever I'd find them on a menu I ordered them. On occasion, I even treated my dinner guests to them. Now, I realize they are the garden-type variety of snail. But with butter and garlic and parsley stuffed into the shells, I just don't think about the garden bit.

Preceding a foray into the woods one morning with the chef and Marjie, we hoisted long, skinny sticks and buckets of sorts, and set out to search for snails. Right off, the chef found a rout of them. We nudged and prodded the sluggish edibles and waited, allowing them to attach themselves to the sticks for a time-dragging stroll up to the bucket. Once we'd pilfered the desired amount, the chef rolled our catch into little cages lined with corn meal, where the snails remained imprisoned for three days—just enough time to clean out their little bodies before abruptly ending their little lives. By the way, the villagers also do their part in denuding the woods (or at least, in keeping down the numbers of the snail population). Needless to say, that woodsy experience—quite eye-opening—has ruined my appetite for snail. And calling it by its French name no longer blocks the images I now carry with me.

Monthly visits have allowed me to see the château blanketed in snow, experience *al fresco* spring dining by the lake, and hike to nearby Vézelay and Beaune in the quietude of early summer. Bastille Day also brought Marjie and me together with the neighboring villagers, who shared their homemade red wine (ouch!). Later, on our stomachs in a nearby field, we watched a very sporadic fireworks display, laughing and counting the minutes before the next *pop* lighted up the sky. Ah, France.

29

After inquiring about certain ways to add to my coffers, I learned that no opportunities are available to Americans unless you are hired by an American firm (discounting 'English as a Second Language' teaching positions). The unemployment rate in France is high. It behooves me then, to come up with a plan to be self-employed and also circumvent the $1500 attorney fee (necessary to draw up legal papers demanded by French law). That's the cost to be self-employed. I don't want to break any French laws, but likewise, my pending idea is not a sure thing and, in fact, could be considered small potatoes. Since the exchange rate is no longer 10*ff*, but about 8*ff* to the dollar, necessity forces me to think of something to improve my financial situation.

I certainly did not expect to be in this position. Not only financially, but after well over a year now, the peak, pinnacle—whatever fulfillment I expected to reach —hasn't happened. But this doesn't stifle my passion whatsoever to keep searching. I've been re-evaluating the options I might naturally excel at, something familiar enough to run with. Only one thing comes to mind.

Earlier in my life in Southern California, I was one of many young women who were taking advantage of a charm and modeling school. The popular schools at that time were heavy on the charm, commencing with the proper way to sit and walk before venturing into proper skin care, dress, and finally, tea room and ramp modeling. By graduation, not a single woman was lacking self-confidence. Eventually, I went on to teach at the school before becoming a professional model.

I remember a young widow in one of my classes (I'll call her Jackie.) whose husband had been killed in the Korean War. Slight of build and rather dowdy looking the day she'd arrived at the school, her demeanor was bereft of confidence; pleasant but non-descript, her features disappeared into a blank canvas, on which we could create a true beauty. After six weeks, Jackie walked across the stage and received her diploma. Strikingly beautiful and radiating poise and assurance. Her demeanor shouted, 'Here I am, world!' I recall pure joy and satisfaction, watching women of all ages as they reclaimed their lives and developed beyond their wildest dreams. Just thinking about it again gives me courage.

Maybe I could create something like that here. Apparently my angels have retrieved and are reintroducing that part of my life. Maybe in the form of a workshop. And maybe this will ameliorate my present situation. Its success would prove both monetarily and spiritually fulfilling. And how *à-propos,* in Paris! —the very birthplace of transformation.

I let the idea rattle around in my brain a few days until it grabbed a foothold. I began working feverishly, preparing for it. And because I had been using

Clinique products for years, I enroll for a training session at the Paris headquarters of Laboratoire de Clinique.

Finally, after long days of brainstorming and planning on paper and holding sessions with my supportive friends, *La Femme Unique* is conceived. Long nights I spend outlining and developing the course and subsequent sessions, all which again seem to flow from my pen, as if rendered by another force:

—as the name suggests, *there are no two people alike. And if we accept that no one looks like us, we must accept our uniqueness, and realize that no one can judge us but ourselves.*

—my program will do more than makeover; it will help women *discover the colors that enhance their own natural beauty* or to *re-do their make-up.*

—will lead women deeper into themselves to *see their inner beauty and walk in it.*

—as each woman comes to *see herself in a different light,* she naturally *develops her own individual way of dressing* and a *confidence of who she is.* I've watched this happen before. I've experienced it firsthand. A woman's personal visual image is beautiful. We will explore fashion too, as it pertains to the individual, not according to trends.

—under *Image,* the course will strive to help *discover the 'new you,' re-define the 'existing you,' and realize your unique fashion sense and have the courage to 'be you.'*

—*visualization* will stress that *'You are what you think. So think beautiful!'* *One cannot create life if one's mind is wrapped around negative thoughts.*

It is for the *Make-up and Skin Care* session that Clinique is more than happy to supply me with make-up and skin care samples. *La Femme Unique* (The

Unique Woman) will consist of a five-week workshop that incorporates my design to help the modern woman of any age to search and realize her own distinct beauty. My preliminary work is finished.

The day is here. Fuchsia pink flyers previously went out to all my friends, along with announcements in the monthly newsletter of the American Women's Group in Paris.

To my anticipation and amazement, *La Femme Unique* launched April, 1986. I would like to say that 'standing in line' was the only way to get into my workshop. *Mais non!* It was sporadic. Very few wanted the whole five weeks. Those who did, like Beryl, had a time problem. Since my sessions were set dates, they interfered with spring vacation or other individual plans. The month of May, especially in France, is a big vacation month. I ended up making adjustments to fit the session to the individual.

The workshop, while not heavily attended, thrived. The course proved very rewarding, and it provided me with the opportunity to take students to the Galleries Lafayette for individual custom shopping. I also felt rewarded in that a seed was sown, and a plan had been nurtured and developed into a full-blown achievement. Once the kinks smoothed out I had a viable project on my hands. I could easily adapt it to fit into a Nordstrom or Macys' curriculum, once I return home. The thought catches in my spirit.

Am I actually thinking about returning to the states? I don't have that niggling of uncertainty or desire to keep seeking. No, I have something solid with this project. But home? No, not yet.

During a subsequent interview with an executive of Galleries Lafayette, he suggested I could have the run of the store for my individual fitting sessions, if I improve my French. Okay then, this means enrolling for the summer course at the Sorbonne. *Wow!* Suddenly, my life has grinded into fourth gear.

During my initial contemplations and then creation of the workshop, another situation was already developing and assured me I would not be bored. It would definitely add to my experience here. I've been asked to tutor the niece of Yves St. Laurent.

30

By what stroke of good fortune even brings me to this point? My thoughts tumble over each other on the bus ride for Neuilly. What will these people be like? Will they accept me?

Located on a tree-lined street, the home is well-maintained though not palatial. I walk the short distance, from the sidewalk along a stone path, surrounded by lawn, to the front door and ring the doorbell.

The door opens, and there stands an attractive and tall, slim woman with long brown hair. Lodged between her fingers a cigarette, pointed to the ceiling from a long holder, and held as naturally as if it had been planted there. Her smile and welcoming manner puts me immediately at ease. I am thankful for that, as she does not speak English. Had it been an awkward or intimidating introduction my French would have faltered, and maybe she would have had second thoughts about hiring me.

Cécile, an ingratiating 13-year-old with dark blond hair and an impish smile, stands by her side to greet me. Hopefully, she will be my student. I expect her to be precocious and to challenge me, coming from such an illustrious family.

After exchanging pleasantries in the living room, Cécile graciously escorts me to her bedroom, which will become our classroom. I stand rooted in the doorway and take in the sight.

Adorning each of her four walls—scattered and pinned here and there by thumb tacks—a myriad of unframed sketches by Yves St. Laurent. Black and whites, coloreds. Each drawing clearly displays his distinctive initials at the bottom. The value of these originals flits through my mind. Here in the bedroom of his niece I find myself engulfed by the spirit of the most famous couture designers of all time.

Bridget makes up her mind and I am hired. I will tutor Cécile in English once a week in this very room. One-on-one with a 13-year-old French girl from an illustrious family…naturally, I have trepidations. What if she doesn't like me after all? Well, I must remind myself how every moment of this French odyssey so far has begun much the same way. What initially concerns me always works out. Works out well, I might add. This isn't the time to be shy. I need to plunge in. Besides, awkward first meetings are perfectly normal.

My weekly sessions with Cécile evolve into a predictable pattern: a brief greeting and conversation with Bridget and then into the warm, familiar atmosphere of Cécile's private gallery—our classroom. Comfortable and not ostentatious, the room becomes a friendly meeting place. The only furniture: a small desk with a chair, a bureau, and a single bed on which we usually sit. But being active and curious, Cécile often likes to stand in front of me and interrogate me in English, then ardently absorb my replies. Sometimes we play games; occasionally, we read together from her French schoolbook or a lesson I've prepared in English. There really is no structure or formality to our lessons. I reason that as long as she is getting the exposure to all aspects of the English language (as I am paid to give her), I can live with this. As yet, I have not mastered the French Rs, and she laughs uproariously when I try over and over not to make a gargling sound. In these moments she is the teacher, and we are both learning.

Petite and cherubim, Cécile exudes enchantment. One day during our frivolous chatter, I looked up to see Bridget standing in the doorway.

"*Excusez moi*," Bridget says. Am I about to get sacked? I wonder… This should be a serious endeavor, and here we are laughing. But surprise! Bridget invites me to stay for dinner—with the family. In a way, I feel this a more frightening undertaking. The parents do not speak English, and visions of making a fool of myself romp through my head. Despite a momentary deluge of self-doubt, it takes just one glance at Cécile and her silent, expressive pleading. *Mais non!* This will not happen. I will not give in to fear. I've come too far for that. Besides, how can I pass up such an honor?

All the French customs come rushing back, and I remind myself to keep my hands above the table and not rest them in my lap. Cécile's older sister and her husband (who both speak English) will arrive within the hour, and I will temporarily have a safety net, since I still have trepidations about my French.

Dinner is simple. Some meat (similar to our roast beef) garnished with fresh-roasted vegetables, followed by a salad of long-leafed greens and a cheese plate. We linger over dinner for what seems like hours. I'm sure the abundant red wine makes it easier for me to understand and express myself. At least, I think adequately. Maybe it's just the wine.

After dinner, Bridget leaves the room and returns with a tape cassette in her hand. It seems this tape (and those like it) is used throughout the French school system for teaching English. The teacher on the tape has a definite British accent, and Bridget wants Cécile to learn English without the accent. I can definitely help with that, maybe with an American accent? I find this very interesting and informative, and here I've been bemoaning the fact that I do not sound French. We finish our dessert of fresh fruit, and I've just spent a very enjoyable evening learning a lot about this family, and they, my adventure in coming to France.

On the bus ride back to my apartment, certainly, I relish various high points of the evening, but I'm also throwing around some ideas for my sister's upcoming three-week visit. This will be a visit she will never forget. I want to fill her time here with memories of more than trips to iconic monuments and art galleries; I want Loraine to feel what it's really like to be living here. Loraine arrives and simply joins me as I go about my routine. She comes with me to each of my workshop meetings. She sits with us during my weekly sessions with Cécile. Even my conversation group welcomes my sister with open arms. For a Saturday adventure, the two of us expand outward for a visit to Versailles, one hour by train. We follow the route Marjie and I had taken to Château de Lesvault. The clear sky and balmy weather makes our first weekend ideal for an *alfresco* luncheon in her honor. We even manage a weekend trip to Nice where she meets my mentor,

Marguerite, and explores my former digs. To conclude Loraine's visit, and to have her meet all the *spokes* of my friendship wheel, Monique graciously opens her home for an afternoon tea. And here we are, two dressed-to the-nines Americans schlepping trays and boxes of goodies across Paris on the metro, because I had the great idea to supply the food. A fitting finale to her visit.

On the day of her departure, I rise from my sick bed with my stuffed-up nose, and bid her a nasally goodbye. She kisses me a teary *adieu*, reluctantly closes the door and hurries down to a waiting cab. I am too stuffed up to cry long.

31

In the latter part of June, Cécile's family prepares to move to their summer home in the South of France. On our last day together there are extra hugs and kisses and picture taking. I don't know that after our time together Cécile spoke English with an American accent or not, but we sure did have fun trying to accomplish that feat. And so this experience of a lifetime concludes.

In fact, summer finds all of Paris *en vacances*. Parisians usually migrate to Nice or other parts in the South during the month of August. Mom and pop *marches* close up. *Laveries* and photo shops are abandoned, and Paris is left to the crazy tourists. I fear that this time of year and a previously stolen visa might create a problem for enrolling in the summer session at the Sorbonne. But having previously completed a semester and knowing there is a visa on file at the consulate, the powers that be grant me permission—provided I be tested for placement, which I take and am relieved to be placed at the intermediate level. This time, I will be attending class inside the Sorbonne itself. I will actually walk through the front door and down its hallowed halls—where Victor Hugo and other notable historic figures have trod, even our own Jackie Onassis.

I climb a wide flight of stairs to enter my classroom. It is much like any other classroom, but with an open window that exposes an unattractive, centuries-old courtyard. Since I will be attending summer school and programmed to remain in the city, it might be fun to explore and live in another *arrondissement*. The opportunity actually presents itself when an acquaintance wants to visit her family in Baltimore. As common practice among friends, I am asked to house-sit for a month. My friend's place is indeed in a different neighborhood, the Fifth Arrondissement.

After spending two arduous days lugging clothes, school supplies, and other personal paraphernalia I might need from one apartment to the other by metro, I'm beginning to seriously question the intelligence of my decision. The apartment has a separate tiny kitchen and one small bedroom, but the building and the neighborhood are run down. The inside lighting is dim. The low ceilings close in on me. But! —there is a television. After all this time away from one, it is a treat to have a T.V., though I miss my clean neighborhood and spacious and airy studio.

It starts as a perfect day. Saturday. Sunny. And I've been invited to a late-afternoon party. I had no clue as to how such a perfect day could end so dismally.

The home is a beautiful two-story structure with balconies that overlook panoramas of Paris. I'm feeling *up* and rather looking forward to having a good time. "Everything is Beautiful" comes to mind, and I'm humming the catchy tune as I make my way to the front door.

Bea, the epitome of the perfect hostess, greets me warmly and takes my hand. Inside I see familiar faces, mostly American. There is also a handful of unfamiliar faces, as Bea escorts me through the chattering group.

Eventually, we stop and stand in front of an attractive blond woman sitting on a couch, who is quietly visiting with another woman in an opposite chair. Bea motions for me to sit down, which I do, right next to the attractive blond. She isn't beautiful attractive, but well-coiffed and put together. As we have obviously interrupted their *tête à tête* the conversation ceases, and both well-coiffed heads turn toward us. Bea makes introductions—finally.

"Marilyn, I'd like you to meet Shirley Evans. Shirley, this is Marilyn Pearsol." I see the hushed movement around me but... *Evans...* Could it be? Surely not. Brad and Bill—Bea's husband—work for the same corporation. *No. No, no, no.* Just a coincidence. I can't jump to conclusions. But in my gut I know.

Bea gets up to greet guests and leaves me here to chat with these ladies. But by now, I am so upset I excuse myself on some pretext to find Bea. She hails Bill and asks him to bring me a drink. *Please!* I am certainly ready for one. Once she finishes greeting guests, I follow her into the kitchen.

"What a great party this is," I say, and, "What nice people..." etc.

"Shirley is separated from her husband." Bea gets right to the point. "But they're trying to work things out. I talked her into coming, she needs to get out." Since I am a new acquaintance with plenty of time on my hands, I could entertain Shirley during her difficult time. *How horribly ironic.*

I mumble something feeble, while my stomach lurches. The truth rushes at me overwhelmingly. *My gawd! This is Brad's wife.* I have to control myself, my emotions. My thoughts crash into each other, so that I make some lame excuse about wanting to visit the buffet table—which does actually look inviting—but how do I mask my emotions so that no one picks up on anything? Thank God, I never told Bea (or Marjie, as she is a friend of Bea's) about Brad.

For I don't know how long, I make inane conversation with friends, hoping they don't notice the change in my demeanor. I avoid further contact with Shirley. Rude? Yes, but I don't care. I won't see her again. I don't have the foggiest idea what to say to her. Obviously, Bea wishes me to be friendly and make Shirley feel welcome. I fail miserably. Here I am with a woman who doesn't know me; and further, whose husband I'm sleeping with.

Married! All those 'out of the way' bistros. They weren't romantic, they were intentionally searched out. He must have just left his wife that first day when I saw him in the agent's office. He hadn't just arrived from the states, as I presumed. And now she might want to work things out? Brad sure doesn't. It all makes nauseating sense. The two of us visiting castles around Paris on a weekend, no pictures of him as I was "far the prettier subject." And this hasn't been just a couple of dates we've had; this has been eight months of feelings, of intimacy, of friendship, of…well…of loyalty I thought. No way will I continue seeing him, and that conversation is yet to be had. And whether right or wrong, it'll be over the phone the next time he calls.

While Brad's betrayal goes deep and has left a great void in my life, I will not allow it to be my 'all-consuming *raison d'être*' while in Paris. My life in France has been and will continue to be a joyous and fulfilling time. I will allow my experience (and yes, that's a good word) with Brad to be remembered as a good, loving, and cherished memory. Nothing more. Okay, truth is, I do want to see him again. Badly. But this has to have a good ending. Was it really a betrayal?

We did deign to live in the present. Of course, it was betrayal. He never gave me the choice to be with a married-but-unhappy man or not. I never would have given him a second glance if I'd known he wasn't free. Maybe he wasn't sure he wanted to stay married and was testing the waters. No, he only appeared free. But I can't just walk away without giving him his say.

Since the party and a later phone conversation with Brad, I agree to meet him one more time. We settle on an obscure place. A small café that borders a neighborhood park.

The minions are through with working for the day and have since scuttled to their burrows for the homeward journey. As it is approaching dusk, the normally-occupied, nearby benches are vacant. Across the park an ornate iron arch indicates the entrance to a metro. How many times did Brad and I meet there? I never knew they were covert meetings. Now I know why he seemed so acquainted with the city. The pieces are coming together, but I'm not interested in the pieces; I'm occupied with living. Loving.

Brad's imposing figure approaches, and desire rushes through me. He wears a light jacket over an open-necked shirt. I can't look at him that way anymore. I can't. We stand facing each other before he lumbers up to me, his eyes bore into mine. I know his heart now, I know this look.

His hands lift to hold my face, and he gazes at me a fathomless look before slowly enveloping me in his arms. I let him gather me in his strength and pull me close. I shouldn't but I do. I reach up under his jacket to wrap my arms around his vibrant, warm body. Not a passionate embrace. A lingering, enveloping, belonging hold for what feels like a taste of eternity. Our heartbeats throb in an unmatched rhythm. No words, only this moment. We had our conversation over the phone. We agreed that we both neglected to be totally honest. In an imperfect love affair we were unable to establish a relationship for the right reasons. Unable to divulge my age or financial situation, fears of inadequacy plagued me. What did I expect? I didn't even know me. As the father of two girls, he was indecisive about reuniting with his wife. He was at a crossroads just as I was. We knew what we had. Not sure where we are headed, but this is still Paris, where mortals— regardless of reason—lose themselves. No words of explanation are necessary.

"I'm sorry," he whispers with tenderness. "I didn't mean to hurt you. What we had was real." *I know that.* He doesn't need to say it.

He draws his lips over my entire face, like a phantom breath barely felt yet stirring. *Just stay here*, my soul pleads. But as tears threaten he draws back and rests his hands on my shoulders—an unforgettable smile on his face.

He turns and walks away. The hollowness engulfs me. How will I survive the coming days, knowing he is no longer going to make me laugh and share my Paris memories? The emptiness hurts. I think partly because I know myself now—I will survive. I will get past this hurt. And that hurts.

32

L ife changes. Not necessarily for good or bad. It just changes. Like the
seasons, my life in Paris is also shifting.

Marjie has since left the chateau and Paris. Rita and her husband have plans
to leave shortly. Beryl is currently vacationing, but soon her husband will be re-
assigned. All my American friends—transplants living in Paris on short term—are
gone, except for Karin. This state of affairs would have inevitably occurred. I'm
finished at school, and receiving my intermediate-level diploma proved
uneventful. The adrenalin rush with studying, attending classes, and interacting
with other students every day is still present, but this next level is *superieur*, and
where will that take me? I need to ponder my next move. Neither Karin nor I have
a definitive plan, so for the time being we'll just be tourists.

Each day we meet, pick an area, and off we go. It seems I still can't get enough of this place. The caves, the *allees*, the hidden haunts…such a different side of life. The *quartiers,* the narrow meandering paths…all so medieval.

One morning, over on a picturesque corner on rue Moufftard, Karin and I sip our *cafe au laits* and not talking really, mostly watching a nearby farmer's market playing out its morning ritual.

The stalls openly display their fresh vegetables and fruit in typically-mounded pyramids. Vendors lounge around. Beside them, their burros stand obediently with wares strapped to their furry sides. Across the way a humbly-dressed man plays a sad violin. His case gapes wide from the ground for any tokens of appreciation. This is life here.

Karin and I spend more days on our feet discovering additional sections of Paris we haven't previously seen. We could walk forever and still not see everything. I know that in a short time I'll be bidding Paris *adieu.* My throat tightens, so I look long and hard at the boulevards and *allees,* imprinting the images to memory. I don't want to forget any of this.

One evening, I happen to be watching *The Thornbirds* on television, but with the dubbed French I can't engage in the story. Bored, I click through the channels and pass a flashing image of an American flag waving against a blue sky. I backtrack to the station.

President Reagan and Nancy are walking along a pier, a slight breeze plays with her hair. Behind them, servicemen dressed in white stand at attention. A close-up of President Reagan speaking. Then the camera pans away from him, over to the Statue of Liberty.

Why is France televising an American event? I continue to talk with myself within the unfamiliar confines of the house I am sitting, listening now to our Naval Band playing "America the Beautiful."

>Oh, Beautiful, for spacious skies,

>For amber waves of grain.

>For purple mountain majesties above the fruited plain.

The camera pans to the American Flag and the Statue of Liberty. The music surges, as if begging me to place my hand over my heart.

>America, America,

>God shed His grace on thee.

>And crown thy good with

>brotherhood,

>From sea to shining sea.

I'm crying now, almost sobbing.

After three years and a 70 million-dollar restoration, the Statue of Liberty is suddenly the center of an extravagant centennial celebration. President Reagan re-ignites the torch of Lady Liberty on July 3, 1986. It was 100 years ago, in 1886, when President Grover Cleveland had accepted this gift from France. And here I am so out of touch with my own country—it seems like forever. Is it time to go home? What else am I seeking here? Nothing comes to mind. But the peace is present as I make my decision. What friends are still here will be gone soon. I have experienced more than I ever could have dreamed possible. Memories are solidly ingrained. I have formed a skeleton of a business. That makes me smile.

Yes, it's time. I'm ready. In fact, I can't wait to wrap things up. It's September already; I'm eager to get back home and continue there with this rejuvenated life and newly-found confidence and purpose. I don't know what awaits me back home, but as when I'd moved in faith to this City of Light, I know I will find my way back again; I will choose the right path for my life. I have reached and attained far more than I ever dreamed possible here. I feel strong. I've mounted the insurmountable! I now have the peace I so desperately sought after. More importantly, I'm walking in peace now. It is said that time heals all wounds. Pain lessens, and new hope is born. But wounds never really vanish, they merely fade and stay tender.

San Francisco

The jetliner skirts the clouds over the Atlantic, and I'm replaying the journey that started almost two years earlier. I am heading home to California with a stopover in Iceland to visit Vally. Excitement builds inside me, and the gears inside my head are churning with plans. I will relocate to San Francisco, instead of southern California. That's a given. Besides, San Francisco is more culturally akin to Paris. Since Vance has graciously invited me to stay with him until I get settled, I really couldn't be more ready. I'm already imagining the steep streets and trolley cars and the diverse sea of humanity. How accustomed I've become to the Parisian leisurely pace. But bistros do not line our streets back home. City life there will not allot for the pondering it takes to consider life, the universe, and the parts we are to play on this field called Earth. I know that I will have to fight to maintain the peace I've since found, as California nurtures a stressed and harried culture.

Reluctantly then, I shuck my longing thoughts of France and shift my focus forward.

Within a month I'm in my own apartment and have put out my antennas for the perfect job opportunity, even enrolling at a temp agency. Anything. Astonishingly—predictably, that is, given my continued luck—after only two weeks I meet the director of convention services and special events for Macys, a Mrs. Marshall, for lunch. A mutual friend who I knew in Paris arranged this meeting, thinking Macys might be interested in my *La Femme Unique* program. I might have known my angels are still with me.

Mrs. Marshall telephones back to tell me about an upcoming event in San Francisco—a panel of four women scheduled to speak on a *'40s, '50s and Fabulous* theme, to be held at the Moscone Convention center and, Would I be interested in speaking in her place and relate my experience in France? Scheduled as one of the speakers, she wasn't able to make it. My first reaction, of course, is how inadequate I feel for such an undertaking. But faith has led me this far... "I would love to," I tell her. This might be the fortuitous moment to introduce my *La Femme Unique* program.

The event proves quite successful. A good report must have found its way to Mrs. Marshall, because she calls again, wondering if I'm interested in coordinating a fashion show in the grand ballroom of the Mark Hopkins Hotel, on Nob Hill the following January—in three months. *Oh, my gawd!* Since I managed to muddle through on the panel, I ponder the thought of enrolling in a public speaking course.

Macys convention services has a spousal program with (just as it sounds) various programs of entertainment for spouses of the conventioneers, and a fashion show appears to be a popular choice. As it was at the Moscone Center. I know the Mark Hopkins show will be a formidable task; it will push at all my experiential boundaries. I don't tell her over the phone that I've never coordinated an entire show, and now is not the time to enlighten her. We'll use professional models and coordinate the music with professional musicians.

The Mark Hopkins show proved successful but costly. Mrs. Marshall questions the cost and how we might cut back next time. With much bravado I proclaim, "Why not use part of my *La Femme Unique* program—fashion as it pertains to women as individuals—as the format? We could use as models some of the ladies who are requesting the show?" I've long advocated the use of nonprofessionals; the vast female population does not identify with extremely tall, sizes four and two, professional models. "This time, we'll use regular women who vary in size and shape. One requirement though: each model must have a true size —six or sixteen—no half sizes, no alterations. Each participant will send a color photo of herself, state her sizes in various apparel and shoes, and state what her hobby is. From these photos, I'll assign each model three outfits." Mrs. Marshall agrees.

Previously, Macys had issued me a badge that allowed me to pick over their racks for our models' accessories. With this badge I had the run of the store, without being hassled by security. It was especially heaven-sent to be free to grab outfits from the *haute couture* section.

So here I am (as in Nice) a kid in a candy store really, draping armfuls of merchandise—forget the security tags!—scurrying from section to section and, of course, triggering alarms. Security guards look over to see that it's just me and pay me no heed. No arrests. When the models arrive we're ready and waiting. I hold my breath, as each participant pulls a garment over her head, tugs at a zipper, steps into pants that were meant to fit like a glove…perfect. I exhale and breathe freely. Next, a practice sashay down the long ramp that juts into the venue—always one of San Francisco's first class hotels.

With the basics completed, the following morning we gathered backstage amid the portable apparel racks, the sections for make-up and hair styling and the smell of hair spray and dressers milling around their models. Imagine my surprise, that while I'd been meeting these models for their fittings, a gorgeous Golden Retriever was posted to the side of a striking, slender redhead who stood 5'7". Her entry photo depicted a demure girl in a print dress, but I instinctively saw this natural beauty in Ralph Loren. I was not mistaken, but a blind girl on the ramp? This would be a challenge. I needn't have worried though, as Jenny and Rusty proved a dream. In practice, I took her hand and gently led her through the routine. But now it's show time.

On my command: "Okay, Jenny," she stops, turns, poses, then continues on. With Rusty by her side she works the ramp flawlessly three times. Jenny turns at the final "Okay," walks back to the podium and turns again to face her audience. The room erupts in applause. Goosebumps race up my arms and down my legs. What Jenny must be feeling right now?

As subsequent models stride onto the stage and see their peers sitting at elegantly-set, white-clothed tables, I know they feel special and beautiful. And they are. My models, beautiful women from all walks of life and of different sizes, hobbies and ethnicity, morphed into vibrant new beings bursting with self-confidence. How regal and proud they stride down the ramp. The applause is a reward from heaven. My plan has worked. We did it! We are on our way.

La Femme Unique continued to touch hundreds of women and guide them into believing in themselves and secure them with their own very unique beauty. The luncheon fashion shows always succeeded, our highest attendance attracting 500 ladies. We played in most of the top-ranking hotels in San Francisco, even Reno, before the curtain finally dropped on this perfect creation, originally manifested during my stay in Paris. My last show was in October, 1989, literally days before San Francisco's Loma Prieta earthquake. What began in a dark place as an impossible dream broke through the surface of doubt and fear, and blossomed. I did find my tomorrow in Paris. The story continues to flourish as the pages of my life keep turning.

Epilogue

As for my friends in France: Marguerite, at 105 years of age, is still living in Nice. I visit as often as possible, and we communicate via friends regularly. Marjie, an established, award-winning artist, flourishes in Colorado. We visit each other occasionally and keep in touch by phone and email. Karin lives in Australia. She visited me in San Francisco and we communicate by phone and e-mail. Vally returned to Iceland. I visited her on my way home from Europe coincidentally during Iceland's 100th anniversary celebration. We keep in touch by e-mail and phone.

Acknowledgments

I like what Tristine Rainer wrote: "You are a not-at-all famous person to whom life has given experiences too valuable to fade into oblivion," and "nearing the end of your life, you write to understand and share what it has meant." This book has been eight years in the making, with thanks to all my school books, papers, calendars, and letters I'd saved. I've come to this place where I can thank the special people who helped make it happen, or who in some way have inspired me. I have used only the first names of my friends mentioned in the book, in addition to the first names of the Yves St. Laurent family. All other names have been changed.

As I mentioned in the book, Marguerite Kaufmann was and is an inspiration to me in my daily life.

I thank Jack Kneise for his original ten-page critique, which turned me in the right direction.

Jane Kalkanian, for her continual support and the tedious task of reading many drafts.

Ann Bogner and Sally Blevins, for their time and energy in reading and critiquing the book.

Marjie, for recalling things I'd forgotten and her continued inspiration.

Jennifer Hamilton, my personal editor, for the endless and time-consuming task of correcting my many flaws. For going inside my head to figure out what I meant to say. Her inspiration and confidence in me kept me going.

My husband, Leo, who was fascinated by this part of my life and wanted me to chronicle it. He read every draft, however laborious, made comments and kept me on track. Leo died unexpectedly in February, 2009.

To my sister, Loraine, and to my brother, Vance, who spent weeks with me in France; their untimely deaths in 2006 prevented them from reading the finished copy of *I Found My Tomorrow in Paris*.

Lastly, without the assistance of my tech-savvy granddaughter, Kimberly, I'm afraid this book would be just a dream in the mind of this tech-challenged author.

Cover design and back cover photo by Kimberly Pearsol.

Made in the USA
Monee, IL
16 September 2022